The Ridg y

A DOG WALKER'S GUIDE

Debbie Kendall & Nigel Vile

COUNTRYSIDE BOOKS
NEWBURY BERKSHIRE

First published 2017

Countryside Books
3 Catherine Road
Newbury, Berkshire

To view our complete range of books
please visit us at
www.countrysidebooks.co.uk

ISBN 978 1 84674 344 3

Photographs by Debbie Kendall & Nigel Vile

The cover picture is supplied courtesy
of VisitWiltshire

Designed by Peter Davies

Produced by The Letterworks Ltd., Reading
Typeset by KT Designs, St Helens
Printed by The Holywell Press, Oxford

Contents

Walk

Appendix

Area map showing location of the walks

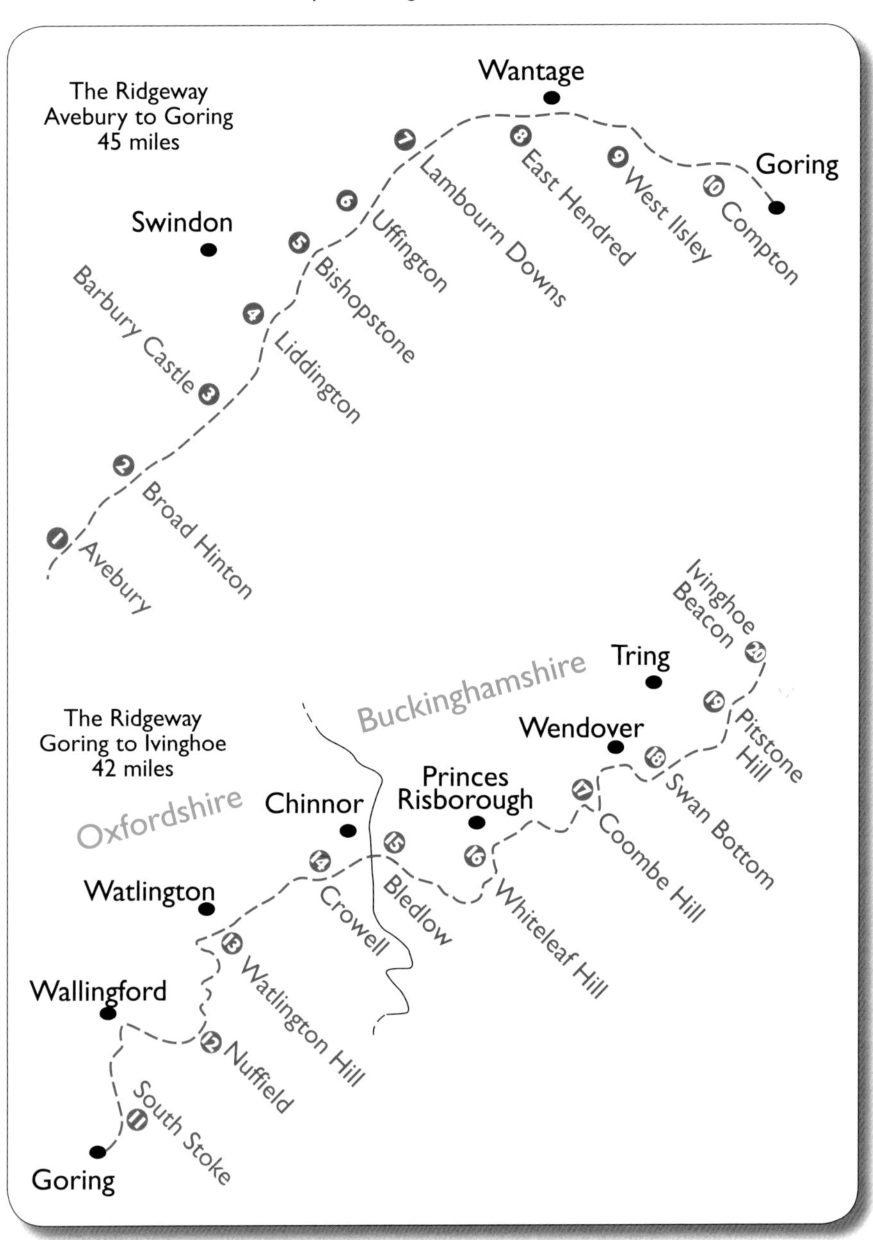

INTRODUCTION

The Ridgeway is a National Trail of 87 miles / 139 km, which follows the route of Britain's oldest road, used since prehistoric times by travellers, drovers and soldiers. It starts at Overton Hill, part of the World Heritage site of Avebury, in Wiltshire, and travels in a north-easterly direction to its end point on the edge of the Chiltern Hills at Ivinghoe Beacon, in Buckinghamshire, some 252 metres above sea level.

The Ridgeway passes through two distinctive landscapes, divided by the River Thames at Goring, in Oxfordshire. To the west, the trail is a broad track, crossing the Wessex Downs, with its wide, open rolling chalk downland and fine views. The trail then rises out of the meadows by the Thames and heads through the wooded hills and picturesque valleys of the Chiltern Hills, often with wonderful views from its chalk grassland hilltops, overlooking the Vales of Aylesbury and Oxfordshire.

Several important archaeological monuments, dating from prehistoric times, lie close to the trail, from ancient earthworks to hilltop forts and figures cut into chalk escarpments. The trail passes by a number of quintessential English villages, many of which boast welcoming, dog-friendly pubs, along with ancient churches, remote hamlets, stunning views, idyllic cottages, imposing country manor houses and delightful nature reserves. But best of all, there's plenty of space for your dog to run free and, while walking the Ridgeway, you'll discover wonderful parts of rural England that lie hidden from our everyday lives.

The 20 walks in this book each take in a section of the Ridgeway and are then made into circular walks, using other footpaths and celebrated trails, for example the Chiltern Way and the Icknield Way. The routes have been developed to give you and your dog the most enjoyable walking experience possible, so road walking is kept to an absolute minimum. England's rich farming heritage means that many of the footpaths criss-cross farmland, so encountering livestock is a possibility on any walk. Please have a look at the dog walker's notes on page 6 for helpful tips on walking safely with your dog in the countryside.

The Ridgeway is generally well-signposted with distinctive black marker posts and signposts, inscribed with an acorn (the symbol of National Trails) and a coloured arrow – normally yellow (footpath for walkers) or blue (bridleway for walkers, horse riders and cyclists).

Debbie Kendall & Nigel Vile

ADVICE FOR DOG WALKERS

All dog owners should be aware of the **Countryside Code** regarding dogs: 'By law, you must keep your dog under effective control so that it does not disturb or scare animals or wildlife. On most areas of open country and common land, known as 'access land' you must keep your dog on a short lead between 1 March and 31 July, and all year round near farm animals.' With this in mind, here are a few gentle reminders.

- Do not let your dog disturb **ground-nesting birds**. Unhatched and young birds will soon die without protection from their parents, and your dog running near the nest might be enough to scare the adult birds away. The nesting period is 1 March to 31 July. Keep your dog in sight and near the path, and don't let him roam into the middle of fields where birds such as skylarks might be nesting.

- Bring **water and a bowl**. The majority of these walks don't pass anywhere where your dog can stop for a drink, so make sure he doesn't go thirsty.

- These walks all pass through **farmland** and the Ridgeway is ideal terrain for grazing **sheep**. The walks each indicate where sheep have been found but fields change their use so keep an ear out as you walk. You can normally hear sheep before you see them. Also check each field before letting your dog loose to make sure there are no livestock. If there are sheep you must always have your dog on a lead. The worry of a dog can cause a sheep to miscarry. Under the Dogs (Protection of Livestock) Act there is a fine of up to £1,000 for worrying livestock, which includes not having your dog on a lead in a field of sheep, even if he doesn't harm them.

- In a field of **cattle**, the advice is different. Keep your dog on a lead and give the cows a wide berth. Be particularly careful if they have calves and if possible avoid walking through the field. But if you find yourself surrounded by a herd of curious cattle, drop the lead and get out of the field. Your dog will be able to escape faster without you. Please also follow any farmers' signs asking for dogs to be kept on a lead.

- **Pick up after your dog**. Please don't leave plastic dog bags lying around. They won't disappear and are dangerous to wildlife. If you are far from a dog bin, pick up a stick and flick it into the hedge where it will decompose and not be trodden on.

- Be aware that the Ridgeway can be used by **motorcycles** and 4 x 4 vehicles from 1 May to 30 September.

- It is a good idea to check your dog for **ticks** after the walk, especially if he has been in a wooded area or in bracken. If you find a tick, you have to remove it as soon as possible. Use tweezers, or better still a special tick remover from a pet shop. Grasp the tick as close as possible to the skin. Then pull the tick straight out without squeezing or twisting it. You can apply products to your dog to prevent ticks and fleas. There are contact details for the nearest vets in the Dog factors box for each walk.

- Finally **look after yourself** by wearing decent walking shoes. Also keep a compass or fully charged smart phone with you to keep an eye on which direction you are walking in, as well as an OS map. The directions have been made as clear as possible, but it is easy to get disorientated in the middle of a wood and there are lots of lovely woods in this book.

Enough of this necessary 'health and safety' detail, the majority of which is simple common sense and courtesy. With minimal road walking, few stiles, and livestock at a minimum, this is a series of walks that we hope both you and your dog will very much enjoy. We wish you many hours of fun and relaxation walking in this beautiful countryside.

PUBLISHER'S NOTE

We hope that you obtain considerable enjoyment from this book; great care has been taken in its preparation. Although at the time of publication all routes followed public rights of way or permitted paths, diversion orders can be made and permissions withdrawn.

We cannot, of course, be held responsible for such diversion orders and any inaccuracies in the text which result from these or any other changes to the routes nor any damage which might result from walkers trespassing on private property. We are anxious though that all details covering the walks are kept up to date and would therefore welcome information from readers which would be relevant to future editions.

The simple sketch maps that accompany the walks in this book are based on notes made by the author whilst checking out the routes on the ground. They are designed to show you how to reach the start, to point out the main features of the overall circuit and they contain a progression of numbers that relate to the paragraphs of the text.

However, for the benefit of a proper map, we do recommend that you purchase the relevant Ordnance Survey sheet covering your walk. The Ordnance Survey maps are widely available, especially through booksellers and local newsagents.

At the time of writing all pubs and refreshment facilities were in business, however, it is a good idea to ring ahead or check online if you are planning on visiting.

1

Avebury

Silbury Hill.

W*orld Heritage status* is not earned lightly and is awarded by UNESCO on the basis of being of 'outstanding universal value'. In the case of Avebury, this also involves 'bearing unique testimony to civilisations that have disappeared', the civilisations in question being the Neolithic and Bronze Age peoples. The sites are many and extend well beyond the well-known stone circle, with its bank and ditch. This area includes a fine stone avenue, any number of barrows, the mysterious mound that is Silbury Hill, as well as Britain's oldest road in the shape of the Ridgeway. It is also the setting that makes Avebury unique, with the village surrounded by Wiltshire's open chalk downland, wide open spaces with big skies and far-ranging vistas. Almost the entire walk is off lead, with field margins and the occasional copse to sniff about in, so you will have a tired and very happy hound by the end of the day.

Terrain

A mix of field margins, enclosed footpaths and wide tracks. There are a couple of moderate ascents along the way, but these bring rewards in the form of wide, expansive views across some of Wiltshire's finest downland.

Where to park

There is a signposted National Trust car park on the southern edge of Avebury, fee payable but free to NT members. (GR 099696). **OS map**: Explorer 157 Marlborough & Savernake Forest.

How to get there

Avebury lies one mile north of the A4 at Beckhampton, on the A4361 road to Swindon. Postcode SN8 1QT.

Nearest refreshments

The Red Lion (☎ 01672 539266) in the centre of Avebury, passed at the end of the walk, welcomes dogs in the front bar or outside on leads. It is open seven days a week and serves food all day. Postcode SN8 1RF www.oldenglishinns.co.uk/our-locations/the-red-lion-avebury

Dog factors

Distance: 6 miles / 9.5 km.
Road walking: The A4361 has to be crossed at the start of the walk, as does the B4003 one mile further on. Dogs should be kept on their leads in Avebury at the end of the walk. Be aware that the Ridgeway can be used by motorcycles and 4 x 4 vehicles from 1 May to 30 September.
Livestock: Sheep often graze within the confines of Avebury's stone circle.
Stiles: None.
Nearest vets: Macqueen Veterinary Centre, 1 Waller Road, Devizes SN10 2GH. ☎ 01380 728505.

The Walk

1. Leave the car park and turn right along the A4361 for 25 yards before crossing over to enter a small enclosure opposite. Dogs can now come off their leads.

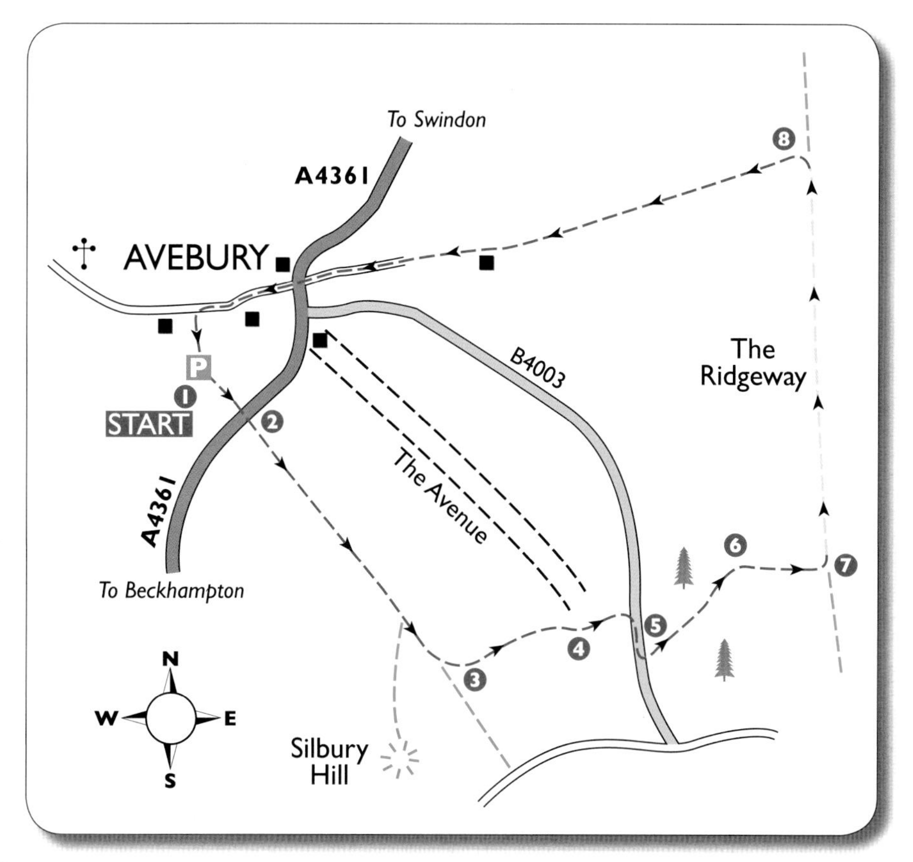

2 Pass through a handgate at the end of this enclosure and follow an enclosed path for 600 yards, alongside the infant **River Kennet** to reach a footbridge on the right and a path leading to **Silbury Hill**. Ignoring this path, continue ahead for 200 yards to reach a gate and open field.

3 Turn left and follow a permissive path that climbs to the top of **Waden Hill**, before descending to reach a gate in the bottom corner of the field at the entrance to the **Avenue**.

4 Turn right and follow the bottom of the field – another permissive path – to reach a handgate on the left in 350 yards.

5 Cross the B4003 – dogs briefly back on their leads - to a handgate opposite and follow another permissive path over to the far right corner of the field ahead. Beyond another handgate, follow a grassy path that climbs uphill to a pair of tumuli covered in beech trees.

6. Continue following the path uphill to a junction by another tumulus and beeches. Turn right and walk for 150 yards to a junction with the **Ridgeway**.

7. Turn left and follow the **Ridgeway** for 1¼ miles to a junction with **Fyfield Down** on the right.

8. Turn left and follow a track – it becomes a lane beyond **Manor Farm** – for 1½ miles to reach the A4361 in Avebury, with dogs back on their leads as you approach the village. Cross over, passing the **Red Lion** on the right, to join Avebury's **High Street**. In 100 yards, having passed the **Henge Shop** and a section of the stone circle on the left, turn left along a path that leads back to the car park.

2

Broad Hinton

Broad Hinton is a pretty village where the church is dedicated to *St Peter ad Vincula* which translates to 'St Peter in Chains'. Only 15 churches in England can boast this dedication, which is in honour of the Basilica of *San Pietro in Vincoli*, in Rome. All around lies open downland, for which Wiltshire is so well known, with big skies and wide expansive views. One of these tracks forms part of the 'White Horse Trail', a 90-mile long distance path that links up the region's famous white horses, including the Hackpen Horse that lies just below the Ridgeway on this walk. Its origin is uncertain. It may have been cut in 1838 by Henry Eatwell, a Broad Hinton parish clerk, perhaps with the assistance of the landlord of a local pub, to commemorate the coronation of Queen Victoria. Dogs will simply enjoy being off-lead and running free along open tracks and grassy paths.

Dog factors

Distance: 5.5 miles / 9 km.
Road walking: There are sections of road walking in both Broad Hinton and Winterbourne Bassett. The A4361 has to be crossed twice along the way.
Livestock: There may be cattle in one field just before the Ridgeway.
Stiles: None.
Nearest vets: Drove Veterinary Hospital, Unit 5 Borough Fields, Royal Wootton Bassett SN4 7AX ☎ 01793 852466.

Terrain

A mixture of grassy paths and enclosed byways. There is one ascent onto Hackpen Hill, which brings its reward in the form of views across vast swathes of Wiltshire countryside.

Where to park

On the green alongside Broad Hinton church (GR 105764). **OS map**: Explorer 157 Marlborough & Savernake Forest.

How to get there

Leave the A4361 Swindon road four miles north of Avebury and follow a minor road into Broad Hinton. On entering the village, turn left in front of a row of whitewashed cottages and follow a quiet back lane along to the church. Immediately past the church is a green with a parking area on the right. Postcode SN4 9PS.

Nearest refreshments

The Crown (☎ 01793 731302) in Broad Hinton welcomes well-behaved dogs. Food is served all day, every day. Postcode SN4 9PA.
www.thecrownatbroadhinton.co.uk

The Walk

1. With your back to the church and facing some properties ahead, turn right and walk across to the far left corner of the green. Pass through a gap in the hedgerow and follow an uncultivated grass strip across the field ahead. On the far side of the field, continue along an enclosed path to reach the road in **Winterbourne Bassett**.

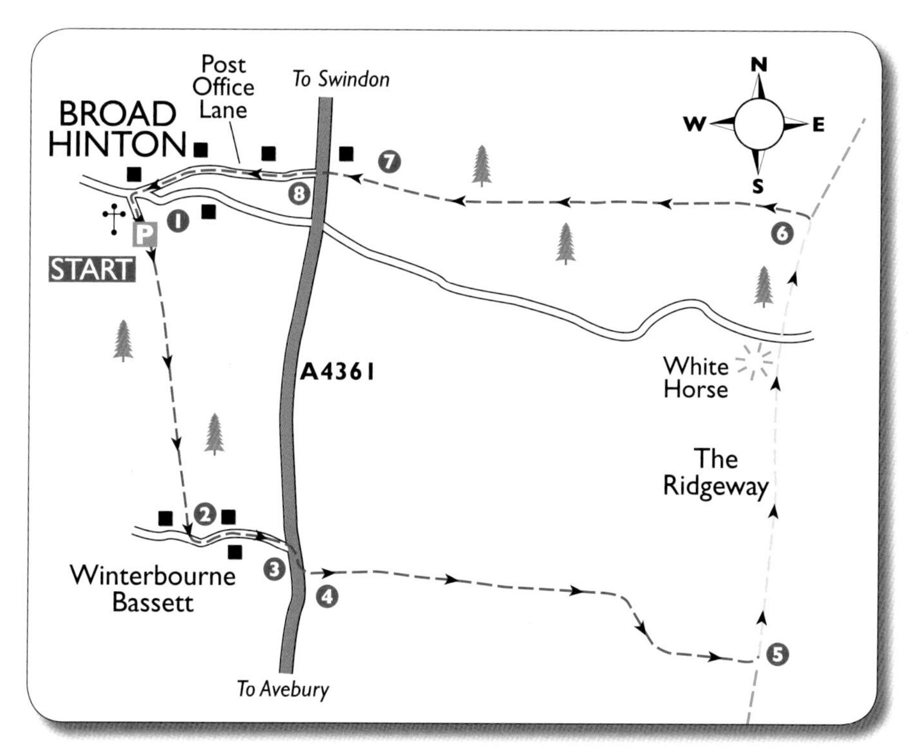

2 Turn left and follow a quiet lane for 600 yards up to the A4361.

3 Turn right and, in 30 yards, turn left onto a gated track signposted as 'Unsuitable for Motor Vehicles'.

4 Follow this track for one mile to a gate and an area of access land. Beyond the gate, follow a path that bears right, climbing the hillside all the while, to reach a gate in the far right corner of the field. Beyond this gate, follow a grassy path ahead that reaches the **Ridgeway** in 250 yards.

5 Turn left and follow the **Ridgeway** for ¾ mile to a parking area on **Hackpen Hill** and a road. Cross the road and continue following the Ridgeway to a clump of beech trees on the left and 150 yards beyond these beech trees, pass through a gateway on the left and follow a bridleway across the hilltop ahead to a gate, with a standing stone on the left.

6 Drop downhill in the next field to reach a gate and a track. Follow this track for ¼ mile, before veering right off the track to follow the signposted bridleway

into a field. Follow the bridleway for ¾ mile as it runs along the left edge of two fields.

7 In the bottom corner of the second field, veer left along a grassy path that passes through a gateway to join the A4361, by the **Barbury Inn**.

8 Follow the road opposite into **Broad Hinton**, reaching the **High Street** in ¼ mile. Turn right and, in a few paces, left along the back lane that leads back to the church.

3

Barbury Castle

Williams Jefferies memorial stone.

Each major town has its 'playground' and the Barbury Castle Country Park fulfils this role for Swindon. This Iron Age hillfort sits high on the Marlborough Downs, where the escarpment drops away to the flatlands of North Wiltshire and more distant Berkshire, encompassing the Upper Thames Valley and the Vale of the White Horse. The walk heads out along the Ridgeway as it crosses Smeathe's Ridge, with wonderful open country and views of some horse gallops, that are far enough away not to bother dogs. The return is by way of enclosed tracks that run through the clay vale, before a climb onto Burderop Down, where we find a memorial stone to Alfred

4

Liddington Hill

Sugar Hill.

This walk, just a mile-or-two from Swindon's south-eastern suburbs, is an absolute classic. From a fairly anonymous layby on the road to Aldbourne, the walk heads out through Shipley Bottom and up onto Liddington Hill, where we join the course of the Ridgeway. In a mile-or-so, there is an almost obligatory detour to Liddington Castle, an Iron Age hillfort with a commanding location high above the North Wiltshire countryside. Stretched out below is the whole of Swindon, with vistas that extend deep into the Cotswolds. The Ridgeway section of this walk ends below Liddington Castle, beyond which lies Sugar Hill, archetypal chalk downland with tumuli, earthworks and barrows. All of this pre-historic detail will be lost on our four-footed friends, who will simply revel in the opportunity to run free along ancient tracks through genuine 'big sky country'.

Terrain

Well-defined tracks that cross open downland. A moderate ascent onto Liddington Hill and a steep descent from Sugar Hill.

Where to park

A parking area alongside the B4192 between Swindon and Aldbourne (GR 231786). **OS map:** Explorer 157 Marlborough & Savernake Forest.

How to get there

Follow the B4192 from Aldbourne towards Swindon. In 3 miles, just before the 'Welcome to Swindon' road sign, a byway crosses the road. At this point, turn left into a parking area at the start of this byway. If this parking area is full, drive along the B4192 for 50 yards and there is a layby on the left. Postcode SN4 0EB (nearest point).

Nearest refreshments

The Village Inn (☎ 01793 790314) in Liddington, on the B4192 heading back into Swindon, allows dogs into its garden. The inn's home-cooked food is, wherever possible, produced using local Wiltshire ingredients. Postcode: SN4 0HE www.villageinn-liddington.co.uk

Dog factors

Distance: 5 miles / 8 km.
Road walking: None, other than crossing the B4192 on two occasions.
Livestock: Occasionally sheep will be grazing on some of the downland fields.
Stiles: None.
Nearest vets: Eastcott Veterinary Clinic, 6 Clive Parade, Cricklade Road, Swindon SN2 1AJ. ☎ 01793 528341.

The Walk

1 Follow the byway, away from the B4192, to reach a junction with the **Ridgeway** on the hilltop in 1 mile. Turn right and follow the **Ridgeway** towards **Liddington Castle**.
(***Detour:*** in 1 mile, a permissive path on the left leads to **Liddington Castle**. Follow the right edge of a field to a gate in its corner before turning left to follow the line of a fence across the hilltop to reach the castle.)

For the main walk, follow the **Ridgeway** ahead as it drops downhill to reach the B4192 in ½ mile.

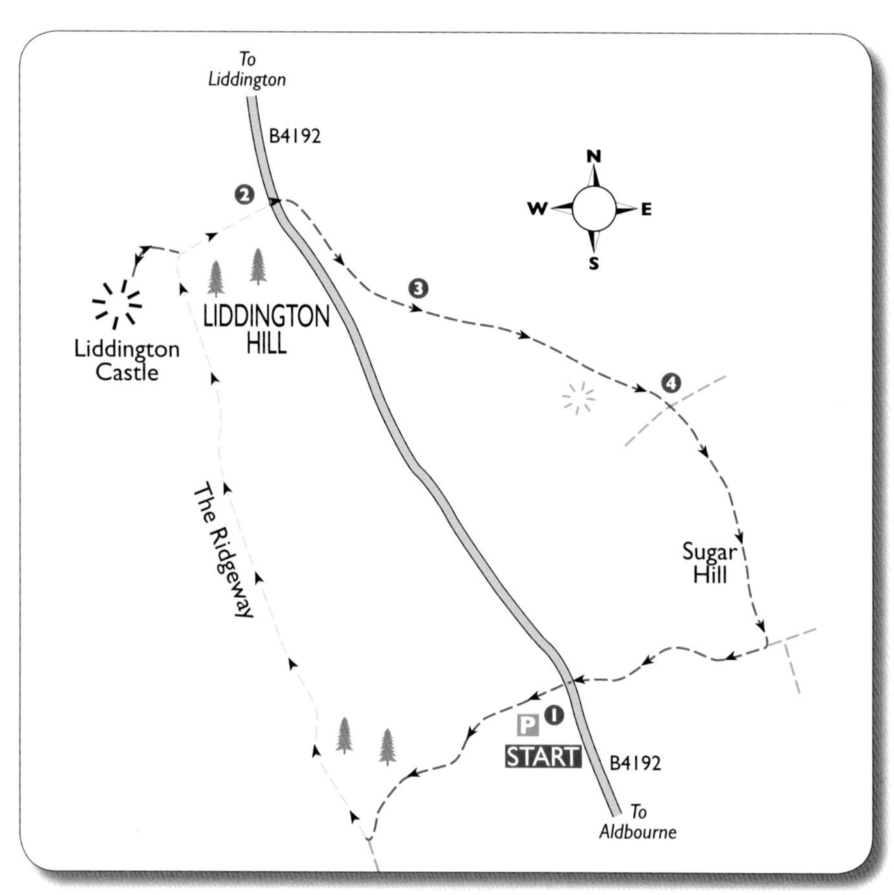

2 Cross the road and pass through a gap in the fence opposite. Turn right and follow the **Aldbourne Walk** as it runs alongside the B4192, separated by a hedgerow.

3 In 600 yards, at the far side of a third field, keep on this path as it bears left away from the main road before bearing right out towards **Sugar Hill**.

4 In ¼ mile, at a crossroads with a bridleway on the left and a footpath on the right, continue following the main grassy path ahead across **Sugar Hill** for ¾ mile to a junction beyond a gateway, where the left turn is signposted to **Aldbourne**. At this point, pass through a gateway on the right and follow a track downhill to reach the B4192 in 600 yards. Cross the road to return to the parking area.

Bishopstone

The village pond, Bishopstone.

Bishopstone is everything that a village should be. There is a school overlooking the village pond, thatched cottages, a traditional village pub and St Mary the Virgin church, where an ornate late-Norman doorway in the chancel once caught the eye of the art historian, Sir Nikolaus Pevsner while writing his renowned *Buildings of England* series. Helen Browning, whose organic brands are distributed nationwide, farms in the village, and her fine products can be sampled at the Royal Oak. A bridleway climbs out of the village, passing through a spectacular gulley in the chalk hills, before reaching the Ridgeway as it runs across the local hilltops. All around lies traditional Wiltshire downland, with ancient field systems and lynchets, testifying to the long history of human settlement in the area. For dogs there is the freedom of being off lead and running free, unencumbered by the threat of traffic.

Terrain

Well-defined tracks and paths. One moderate climb out of Bishopstone and a descent from the hills into Idstone.

Where to park

The church car park in Bishopstone (GR 243838), although avoid parking here when services are on. At such times, park on the roadside in the centre of the village near the pond. Opposite is Church Walk as mentioned at the start of the walk. **OS map:** Explorer 170 Vale of White Horse.

How to get there

At the Swindon end of the village, follow West End Lane signposted to 'Church Car Park'. In 50 yards, turn right into Church Lane. The car park is at the end of this lane on the left. Postcode SN6 8PY.

Nearest refreshments

The Royal Oak (☎ 01793 790481) in Bishopstone 'loves its customers whether they have dogs, kids, muddy boots or soaking wet anoraks'. Being owned by Helen Browning of organic food fame, expect some fine food offerings. Postcode SN6 8PP www.helenbrowningsorganic.co.uk/pub

The Walk

1. Leave the car park, turn left and walk up to the village church. Follow the path to the left of the church and out onto **Church Walk** before continuing up to the main road in Bishopstone.

2. Turn right and follow a path alongside the road to the entrance to **Prebendal Farm**. In another 25 yards, cross the road and follow a bridleway opposite. In ¼ mile, beyond a gate, continue following the bridleway uphill through a shallow valley for 350 yards to the next gate. Continue following the bridleway uphill to the next gate and the **Ridgeway**.

3. Turn left and follow the **Ridgeway** for ¼ mile to a crossroads by **Ridgeway Farm**. Continue ahead on the **Ridgeway** for another mile to the next crossroads by another farm.

4. Turn left and follow **Idstone Hill** downhill to a junction in just over ½ mile.

5. Turn left and, in a few paces, right, down a back lane into **Idstone** village. Follow this lane, it bears left and then right, for 200 yards down to **Lower**

Dog factors

Distance: 4 miles / 6.5 km.
Road walking: Short sections in Bishopstone and Idstone. The descent into Idstone is along a cul de sac lane that is only used by the very occasional farm vehicle.
Livestock: Occasionally in the fields above Bishopstone and on the return from Idstone to Bishopstone.
Stiles: None.
Nearest vets: Eastcott Veterinary Clinic, 6 Clive Parade, Cricklade Road, Swindon SN2 1AJ. ☎ 01793 528341.

Idstone Farm. Turn left along to a gate, passing some barns, before continuing ahead to another gate and a field.

6 Walk across this field, bearing right all the while, to a point where a hedgerow forms a corner just past a telegraph pole. Beyond this point, turn right and walk down to a gate in the bottom corner of the field. Cross a stream and

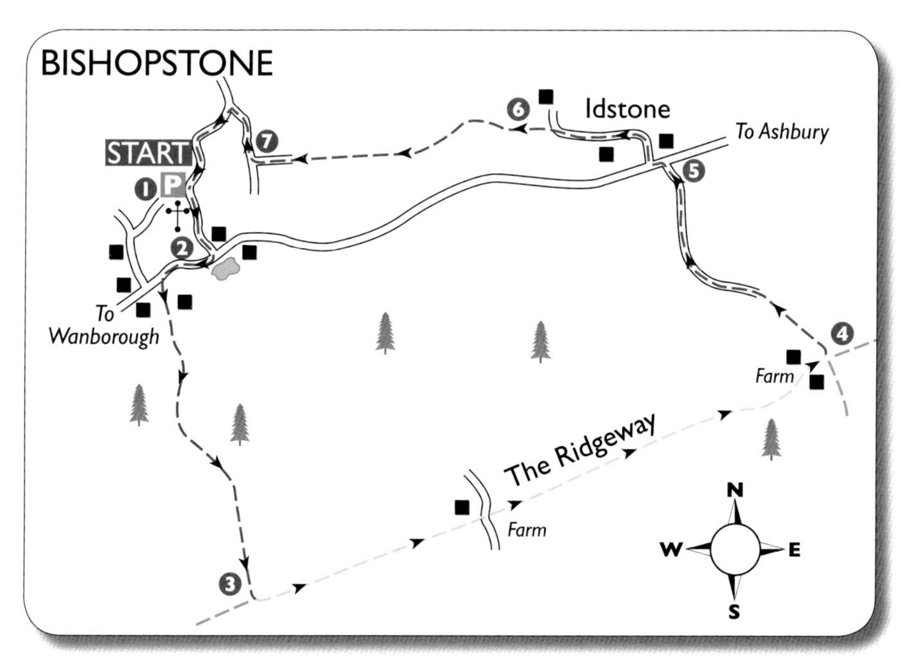

follow the left edge of the next field for 100 yards to a gate and an enclosed path. Follow this enclosed path for ¼ mile to a quiet lane on the edge of Bishopstone.

7 Turn right and, at a junction in 150 yards, turn left to walk into **Bishopstone**. In 200 yards, by a property called **Crookhollow**, turn right into **Cues Lane**. In 150 yards, on a left-hand bend by **Eastbrook Farm**, keep ahead on a path that passes **Cues Farmhouse**. Once past the farmhouse and its grounds, cross a footbridge on the right that crosses a stream. Continue along this path to **Church Lane**, where the car park is on the right.

6

Uffington

The White Horse.

Travellers have been making their way up and down the Ridgeway for over 5,000 years, making it Britain's oldest road. It comes as no surprise, therefore, to find many ancient landmarks in the vicinity of this time-honoured track, and this walk can boast no fewer than four genuinely iconic landmarks. There is Wayland's Smithy, a Neolithic chambered long barrow, that was once believed to have been the home of Wayland, the Saxon god of metal working. This atmospheric site lies one mile along the Ridgeway from Uffington Castle, an early Iron Age hillfort whose banks and ditches cover a site of 32,000 square metres. Below the hillfort, lies the Uffington White Horse, whose well-known skeletal outline dates back over 3,000 years. And facing the white horse is no less than Dragon Hill, an oddly-shaped but distinctive hillock where St George allegedly slew the dragon. A bare patch of chalk on this hillock, a patch where no grass will grow, is purported to be

The Lambourn Downs

For most walks, a paragraph of descriptive prose is all too easy to write. There are villages with ancient churches and traditional pubs, old tracks bordered by long barrows or hillforts ... in other words, history and intrigue at every turn. This walk is, to quote a well worn phrase, 'something completely different'. It is a lengthy excursion across an open landscape almost devoid of human settlement other than the occasional farm. The OS map refers to this area as 'The Lambourn Downs' which, most experts agree, offer excellent walking with wide open vistas over rolling countryside. Lambourn has also been labelled as 'The Valley of the Race Horse' and, on this walk, you might spot next weekend's runner at the 2:30pm at Kempton in training! Our four-footed friends will, once clear of an initial section of potentially busy road, revel in this wide open landscape.

Dog factors

Distance: 7 miles / 11 km.
Road walking: There is an unavoidable section of road walking alongside the B4001 at the start where dogs must be on leads. Beyond the B4001, there are occasional farm roads accompanied by grass verges. Just be aware of any vehicle noise.
Livestock: None.
Stiles: None.
Nearest vets: Abivale Veterinary Group, Belmont Surgery, Belmont, Wantage OX12 9AS ☎ 01235 770333.

Terrain

Well-defined tracks throughout. The landscape is gently undulating so there are no significant ascents along the way.

Where to park

A car park on the Ridgeway close to Hackpen Hill (GR 344851). **OS Map:** Explorer 170 Vale of White Horse.

How to get there

The Ridgeway crosses the B4001 midway between Wantage and Lambourn. There is a parking area to the east of this main road alongside the Ridgeway. Postcode OX12 9XE (nearest point).

Nearest refreshments

This walk is in a remote location with no nearby pubs. Drive to Letcombe Regis, however, and you will find the dog-friendly Greyhound Inn (☎ 01235 771969). An 18th-century free house, where all the food is homemade, freshly cooked and based on local ingredients. Postcode OX12 9JL www.thegreyhoundletcombe.co.uk

The Walk

1. Leave the car park and turn left, walking along a verge beside the often busy B4001 for ¼ mile.

2. Then turn left onto a private road – it is a public byway – signposted to **Greendown Farm**. Follow the grassy ride alongside this very quiet farm road for just under 2 miles to reach **Sheepdrove Farmhouse**. Continue for 600 yards to reach a junction by a barn and the entrance to **Sheepdrove Natural Burial Wood**.

3. Turn left and follow a farm road for ½ mile to a point where it bears left

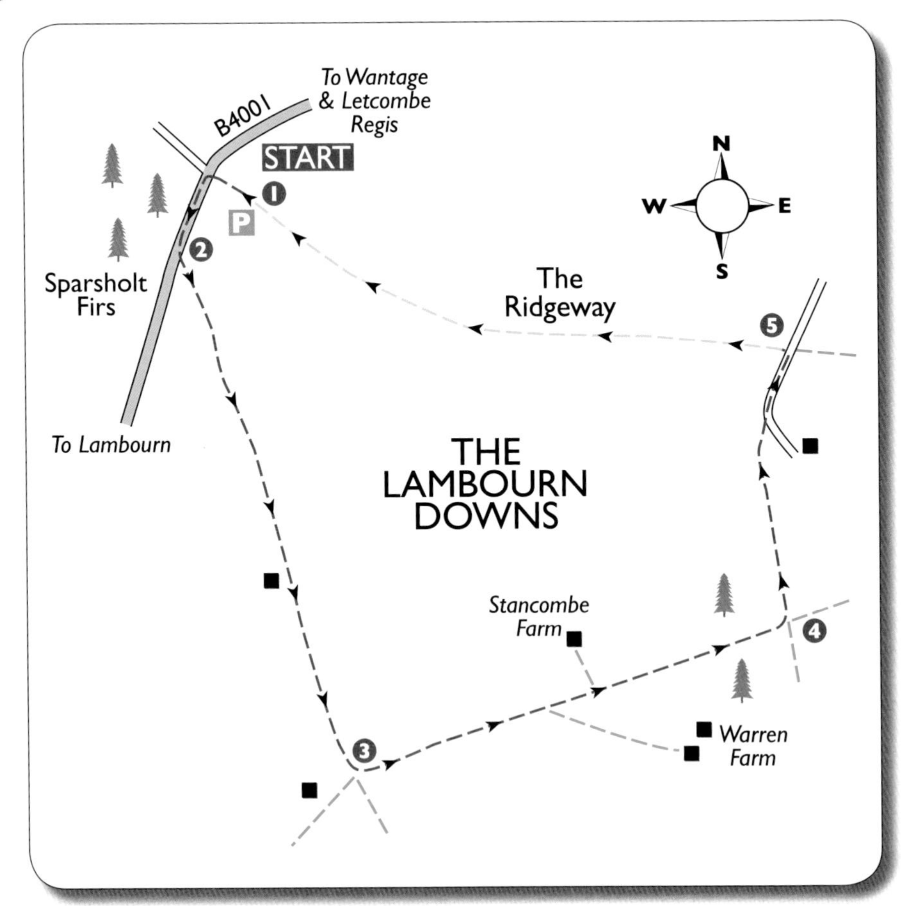

Sheepdrove natural burial wood.

towards **Stancombe Farm**, ignoring a right turn to **Sheepdrove Organic Farm** along the way. At this point, keep ahead on a byway and continue for 1 mile to reach a junction of tracks.

4 Turn left and follow a byway for ¾ mile to reach a junction with the **Ridgeway**.

5 Turn left and follow the **Ridgeway** for 2 miles back to the car park.

8

East Hendred

St Augustine's church.

Leaving the nearest main road at East Hendred, it takes over two miles of driving along an ever narrower road to access the parking area for this remote Ridgeway walk. Along the way lies just one property whose name – Land's End Cottage – simply says everything. All around lies open downland, with fine views and open vistas. That the ancients came this way is evident from Scutchamer Knob, located in a small area of woodland by the Ridgeway. Also known as Cuckhamsley Hill, this raised earth mound is an early Iron Age round barrow. Legend maintains that this was the burial place of the Saxon king Cwichelm. Scutchamer Knob was excavated and ruthlessly dug away in 1842, which has given it the shape of a crescent moon, or a croissant, depending upon your imagination. For 'peak baggers', there is also the trig point on Cuckhamsley Hill - these white concrete pillars may well have become redundant in this era of satellite navigation, but trig pillars are quintessentially British, and even made it on to Bill Bryson's list of favourite British items in his bestseller, *The Road to Little Dribbling*. As for our four-footed friends, this corner of Oxfordshire will be a landscape where they can simply run unencumbered and free.

Dog factors

Distance: 4 miles / 6.5 km.
Road walking: A very short section of road walking before Land's End Cottage.
Livestock: Watch out for sheep in fields adjoining some of the tracks.
Stiles: None.
Nearest vets: Abivale Veterinary Group, Belmont Surgery, Belmont, Wantage OX12 9AS ☎ 01235 770333.

Terrain

Well-defined tracks throughout. The landscape is gently undulating so there are no significant ascents along the way.

Where to park

A car park on the Ridgeway at Cuckhamsley Hill (GR 458850). **OS Map:** Explorer 170 Vale of White Horse.

How to get there

Leave the A417 in East Hendred, 4 miles east of Wantage, and follow White Road, signposted to East Hendred village and the Eyston Arms. Having passed through the village, follow what becomes a rough cul de sac lane for 2¼ miles until it reaches the Ridgeway on the hilltop. Turn left into a parking area. Postcode OX12 8QU.

Nearest refreshments

Well-behaved dogs (and ramblers!) are welcome at the Eyston Arms (☎ 01235 833320) in East Hendred. The fish specials are excellent, on account of the inn's contacts with small-scale inshore fishermen. Postcode OX12 8JY www.eystons.co.uk

The Walk

1. Walk back to the crossroads where the **Ridgeway** joins the lane to East Hendred and follow the restricted byway to the south, away from the **Ridgeway**, for 1¼ miles.

2. When you come to a junction with a road, turn right and walk towards a property called **Land's End Cottage**.

3. Immediately before this property, turn right onto a restricted byway. At the rear of this property, veer left off the main chalky track to follow a grassy path that runs parallel to – but below – the track. Follow this grassy track for ½ mile to a crossroads, before continuing ahead on a grassy path that runs between woodland. In ½ mile you come to the **Ridgeway**.

4. Turn right and follow the **Ridgeway** for 1½ miles back to the parking area. As you return to the parking area, the trig point on **Cuckhamsley Hill** is on the left, and Scutchamer Knob is on the right.

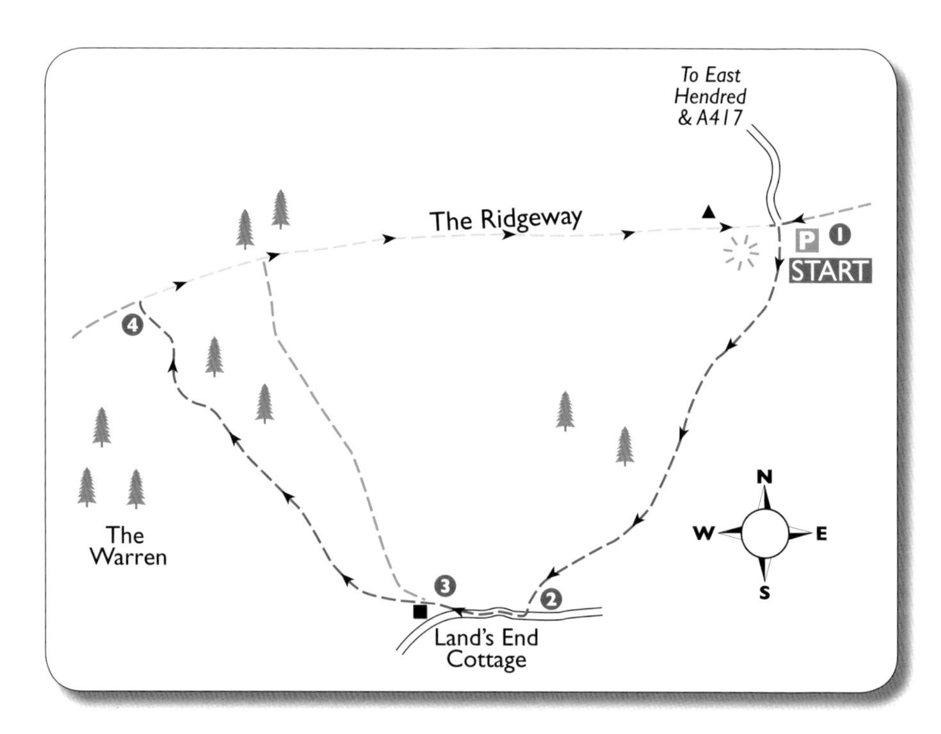

West Ilsley

In *The Berkshire Book of Song, Rhyme and Steeple Chime*, written by Arthur Humphreys in 1935, the following verse appeared:

Ilsley remote amidst the Berkshire Downs
Claims those distinctions o'er her sister towns
Far famed for sheep and wool though not for spinners
For sportsmen, doctors, publicans and sinners.

From the church porch.

6 Turn sharp right along this bridleway and, in 100 yards, turn left onto a footpath. Follow this enclosed path for ¼ mile to a barn and a road.

7 Cross this road and follow the footpath opposite, keeping left in 150 yards to drop down to West Ilsley's '**Main Street**'. Turn right, back to the pub and your parking spot.

Compton

Compton, a station along the Didcot, Newbury & Southampton Railway, closed in 1962. This train line was a crucial transport link during the Second World War, carrying huge numbers of troops south in preparation for D-Day. Compton is also the home of the 'Institute for Animal Health', which explains some of the mysterious buildings around the village! A very gentle climb from Compton brings the walk to the Ridgeway, where once again there are nearby gallops on Compton Downs. This is delightful open countryside, with unimproved chalk downland at every turn, where dogs will enjoy running free under big skies. The walk returns to Compton by way of more enclosed tracks, bounded by hedgerows and woodland, with plenty of interesting sounds and smells for our four-footed friends to investigate.

11

02/06/22

South Stoke

Starting in the lovely village of South Stoke, this walk follows a riverside section of the Ridgeway. It meanders alongside the Thames to neighbouring North Stoke, before looping back through open fields, past Littlestoke Manor. It's a level, undemanding walk with plenty of places for your dog to take a dip in the river on the first leg and a lovely village pub, the Perch and Pike in South Stoke, awaiting you at the end.

Terrain

Away from the Chilterns in the Vale of Oxfordshire, there are no hills on this section of the Ridgeway. The walk is an enjoyable stroll along the river and over open farmland, although there is little shade along its length. There are quite a few muddy stretches in the winter and after prolonged wet weather.

Where to park

There is parking along the verge by the church in South Stoke village. (GR 598835) **OS map:** Explorer 171 Chiltern Hills West.

How to get there

South Stoke is off the B4009 between Wallingford and Goring. From Goring, head north on the B4009 and after about 1.5 miles / 2.5 km turn left into Ferry Road, signposted to South Stoke. Go under the railway line and after 200 m, turn left into The Street, where you'll be able to park on the verge, on the left near the church. Postcode RG8 0JS.

Nearest refreshments

The Perch and Pike (☎ 01491 872415) in South Stoke is a 17th-century inn and converted barn with a selection of real ales and craft beers plus fresh, seasonal, home-cooked food. You'll find it on The Street, just past the church. Postcode RG8 0JS www.perchandpike.co.uk

Dog factors

Distance: 4.5 miles / 7 km
Road walking: 300 m through South Stoke and 125 m through North Stoke plus a stretch of very quiet lane leading to Littlestoke Manor.
Livestock: Cattle can be grazing in the fields by the river after the Four Arches railway bridge and after Littlestoke Manor.
Stiles: 3 – The stile by Littlestoke Manor is not very dog friendly as it is in a section of wall about 1 m high with a rough stone step. My dog (medium size) was happy to scramble over it and smaller dogs can easily be lifted over, but larger and/or older dogs may struggle. The other two wooden stiles are suitable for all dogs.
Nearest vets: Goring Veterinary Centre, 17C High Street, Goring-On-Thames, RG8 9AR ☎ 01491 873638.

The Walk

1. From the church in **South Stoke**, head back up the road (with the brick/flint wall on your right) to the junction of **The Street** and **Ferry Road/Ferry Lane**. Turn left along **Ferry Lane**, following a black signpost for the **Ridgeway**. After 170 m, at the fork, keep left – following the **Ridgeway** along the track to the river.

2. At the river, turn right through the gate and follow the path along the riverbank. Keep going and after about 1 km, you'll pass under one of the four impressive arches of **Moulsford Railway Bridge**. Engineered by Brunel, the bridge carries the busy Great Western mainline from London to Wales. Keep going along the riverbank, through various gates, until you reach a black **Ridgeway** signpost at a boathouse.

3. Turn right here and then, after 50 m at the next signpost, turn left, still on the **Ridgeway**. Now keep going ahead, through several gates, on the path for a further 1 km, until the path runs along the riverside gardens of a few houses at **North Stoke**.

4. Go through the gate into the churchyard of **North Stoke church** and out the other side into **Church Lane**, by a black barn. Follow the lane for 75 m and at its end, turn right (now leaving the Ridgeway) along **The Street**.

5. After another 75 m, the lane bears sharp left, but keep straight ahead here on **Pickets Lane**. Keep ahead, with the hedgerow on your right, between arable fields. After about 850 m the track meets a lane. Keep straight on here, along the lane. A further 275 m on, at the S-bend, keep straight on, past the driveway to **Little Stoke House**. After a further 350 m, alongside a beautiful flint wall, you'll arrive at the driveway to **Littlestoke Manor**.

6. In front of you, in the corner by the green signpost, cross the stile built into the wall. Follow the path ahead for 60 m. Depending on whether there are cattle grazing in the field ahead, you will be directed over 1 of the 2 stiles here. Follow the path ahead along the edge of the field. Go over the next stile at the edge of the field and cross the wooden footbridge over the brook. Now keep ahead across the next field, towards the railway line. As you approach the railway, the path bears left into the next field and you'll soon see a small underpass on your right.

7. Go through the underpass and follow the path as it bears left across the field (under the power lines) towards the trees. The path then runs along the tree-

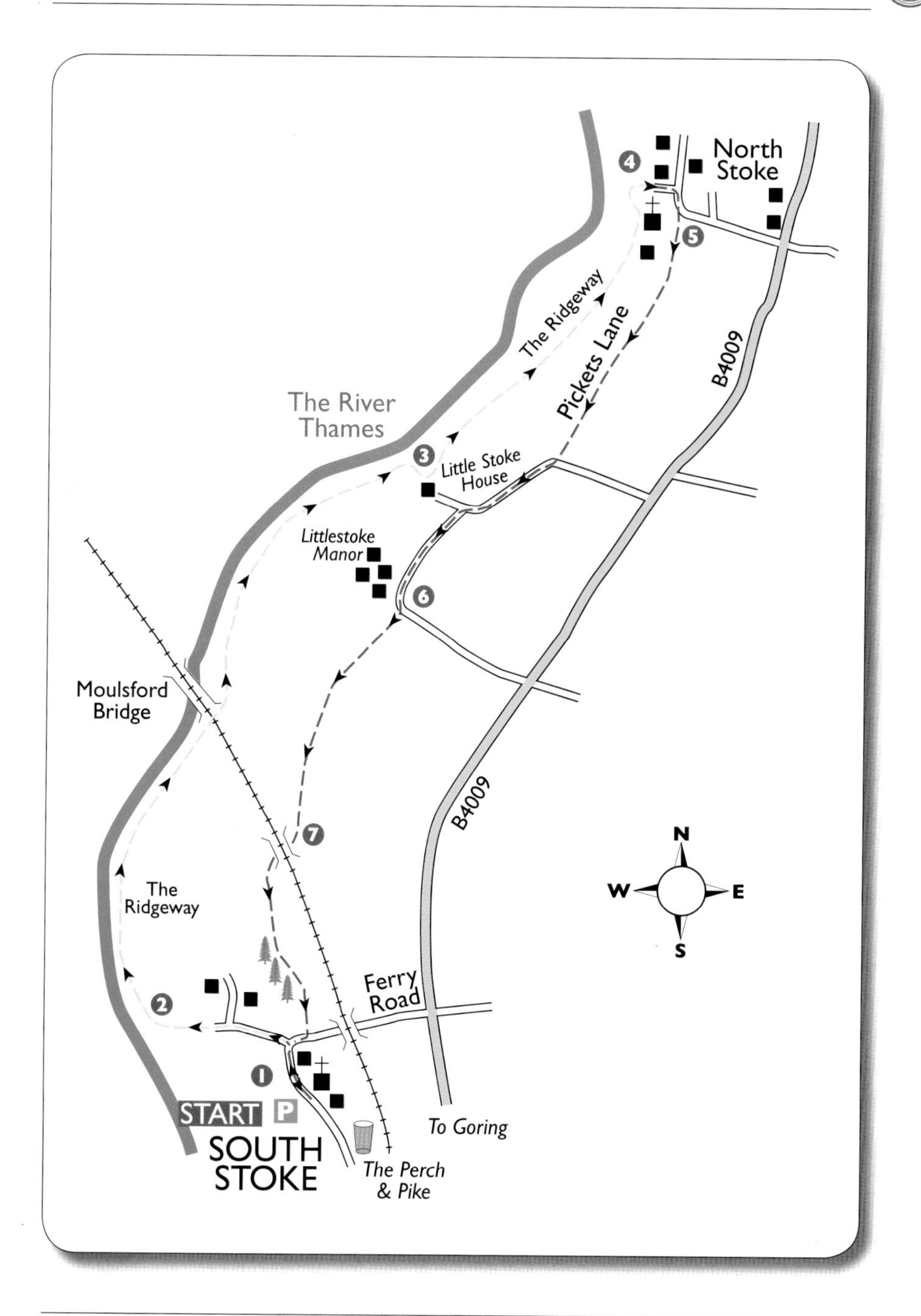
North Stoke
4
5
The Ridgeway
Pickets Lane
B4009
The River Thames
3
Little Stoke House
Littlestoke Manor
6
Moulsford Bridge
B4009
7
N
W
E
S
The Ridgeway
Ferry Road
2
1
START
P
SOUTH STOKE
To Goring
The Perch & Pike

Moulsford Railway Bridge.

line towards a house in the corner of the field. At the signpost, follow the footpath, past the house on your left, to the track. Continue down the track for 60 m where it meets **Ferry Road**. Turn right here and after a further 60 m at the road junction, turn left down **The Street** and back to the church.

Nuffield

This lovely walk has some fine, far-reaching views over the Vale of Oxfordshire and is mostly fairly level. It starts on the Ridgeway as it crosses the immaculate fairways of Huntercombe golf course and then follows the linear Grim's Ditch for almost 2 miles. Dating from the Iron Age, this is a delightful track that both dogs and humans will enjoy, meandering amongst ancient trees with tangled roots. There are a number of 'Grim's Ditches' across England and though there is much speculation about the origin of the name and the exact purpose of these earthworks, they are thought to represent territorial land divisions. The route loops back via the tiny hamlet of Hailey, where the King William IV pub offers a welcome break, before the return leg.

Terrain

The route is fairly level throughout with one gradual incline after leaving the hamlet of Hailey. The route traverses woodland and open fields and many of the footpaths are tree-lined. The walk starts and ends on the fairways of Huntercombe golf course, where dogs need to be under control.

Where to park

Park off the A4130 in Nuffield (GR 675877). **OS map:** Explorer 171 Chiltern Hills West.

How to get there

From Henley on Thames, take the A4130 heading north-west towards Wallingford and Nettlebed. Go through Nettlebed and after about 2 miles / 3 km (shortly after the signposted turns for Nuffield village) turn left into the parking area for the Crown pub (now closed). Postcode RG9 5SJ.

Nearest refreshments

En route is the King William IV (☎ 01491 681845), a country pub in a delightful location in the tiny hamlet of Hailey, with plenty of garden space, real ales and home-cooked food on offer. Postcode OX10 6AD
www.brakspear.co.uk/pub-finder/king-william-iv

Dog factors

Distance: 7.5 miles / 12 km
Road Walking: 3 short sections of road along very quiet lanes: 100 m by Nuffield church, 400 m at the end of Grim's Ditch and 420 m in Hailey.
Livestock: Sheep grazing in the field near Homer Farm.
Stiles: 1 – suitable for all dogs.
Nearest Vets: Abivale Veterinary Group, 16 Queens Avenue, Wallingford OX10 0ND ☎ 01491 839043.

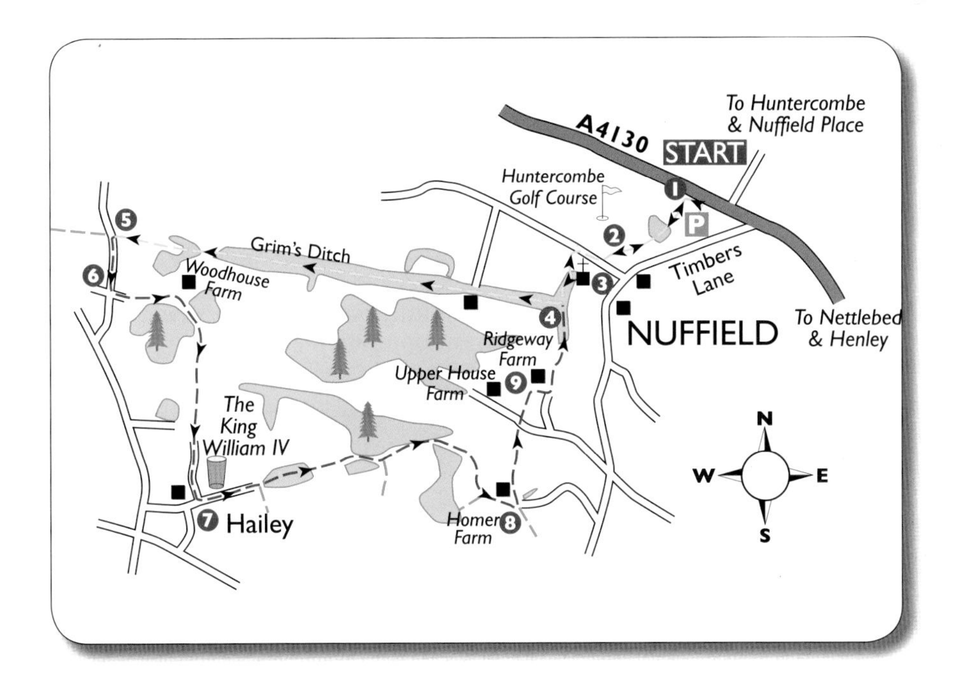

The Walk

1. Start by the (now closed) **Crown pub** off the A4130 at Nuffield. Facing the road, turn left along the track running parallel to the road. At the black signpost, keep straight on (**Ridgeway**) passing in front of the cottages (on your left) then bearing left after the last cottage, to the black marker post at the edge of **Huntercombe golf course**. Keep straight on here, crossing successive fairways and following the black marker posts (with yellow arrows and acorn). You'll go through a copse and, across the next fairway, you'll soon see the clubhouse ahead.

2. Pass around the right-hand side of the black barn-style building – following the black marker post as the path heads diagonally right across the field, through a gate then straight ahead, across the next field towards the church.

3. At the road, by the black signpost, turn right, passing the church on your left, and walk for about 100 m. At the telegraph pole, turn left through the gate into the field, following the **Ridgeway**. Follow the path along the left-hand edge of the field and then straight on, along a wooded path to the next black signpost.

4. Turn right at the black signpost (for **Ridgeway** and **Grim's Ditch**). You now follow the **Ridgeway** for almost 2 miles – keeping straight ahead at the various marker posts and signs along the way. Towards the end of this section the path emerges from the woodland, to run along the right-hand edge of a field.

5. At the lane, by the signpost, turn left – leaving the **Ridgeway** – and walk along the road for about 350 m.

6. At the signpost, turn left (**Chiltern Way**) along the driveway to **Woodhouse Farm**. Follow the track ahead, and almost opposite the farmhouse, turn right (between 2 barns, signposted **Chiltern Way**) onto the footpath heading uphill.

At the top of the hill, the path crosses a track (into private woodland) where the path continues, bearing diagonally right at the marker post. Keep going ahead – out of the woods, across a field and on, along a wide grassy track between open fields, passing two large barns. The track eventually emerges at **Stone Farm**, at a T-junction, in the hamlet of **Hailey**.

7 Turn left along the lane, passing the **King William IV pub** on your left, and go straight on up a tree-lined track with a long gradual ascent. Towards the top of the hill the track enters woodland. Keep going ahead on the main track (purple arrow on marker post) through the woods. Then bear left at the intersection of tracks (following the purple arrow) on the path that runs along the edge of the wood, with an open field on your right. The track then emerges from the woods, soon passing a country house set back on the right, then, downhill to **Homer Farm**, about 400 metres further on.

8 Just past **Homer Farm barns**, turn left at the signpost (Nuffield 1.5 miles) along the track. Keep straight ahead uphill through the garden to a gate at the top. Go through the gate and then straight on through the field (there may be sheep grazing here) – following the line of telegraph poles. Keep going, through the next arable field, across a track, then straight on again, across another field, to a large house (**Ridgeway Farm**) ahead of you.

9 At the farm, at the edge of the field, turn right and then after about 80 m go over the stile and cross the driveway to follow the footpath ahead, alongside the yew hedge. Now keep straight ahead, through a copse, alongside a field and then straight on, back into woodland, where after about 300 m you'll arrive back at the **Ridgeway** signpost to **Grim's Ditch** at Point 4. Now re-trace your steps back to the start.

Watlington Hill and Swyncombe

This beautiful walk takes in some of the best and most varied countryside in the Chilterns. It starts from the top of Watlington Hill, a stunning National Trust chalk downland site with wonderful views across Oxfordshire. There's plenty of open space here for dogs to run free as red kites swoop and soar on the breeze. It then drops down into quintessential English countryside – a mixture of open fields, ancient woodland, sunken bridleways, an 11th-century church and the idyllic rural hamlet of Swyncombe. The full walk is 8.5 miles / 14 km and there are several hill climbs and corresponding descents, but it can easily be split into 2 shorter walks if required: Watlington Hill only (2 miles / 3.5km) or the Swyncombe & Cookley Green loop only (5 miles / 8 km).

Dog factors

Distance: Whole Walk: 8.5 miles / 14 km
Watlington Hill walk only: 2 miles / 3.5 km
Swyncombe & Cookley Green loop only: 5 miles / 8 km
Road Walking: Approx 500 m at Cookley Green.
Livestock: Yes, sheep grazing on the route out of Swyncombe and livestock may be in the fields from Point 13. Game birds will be present in the woods and fields during the shooting season.
Stiles: None
Nearest Vets: Crossroads Veterinary Centre, 36c Couching Street, Watlington OX49 5QQ ☎ 01491 612799.

Terrain

Open chalk grassland on Watlington Hill combined with footpaths and bridleways in open fields and woodland, some of which will be muddy in winter and after wet weather. There are several ascents and descents of varying severity and if you've parked on top of Watlington Hill, you'll need some energy at the end of the walk for the long, but relatively gradual, ascent back to the car park.

Where to park

Option A: For the whole walk or Watlington Hill only walk:
There is a car park off Hill Road, at the top of Watlington Hill, near Christmas Common (GR 710935). **OS map:** Explorer 171 Chiltern Hills West.
Option B: For the Swyncombe and Cookley Green loop only:
There is parking on the verges (towards the bottom of Britwell Hill) on Britwell Hill Road, the lane between Britwell Salome and Howe Hill where the Ridgeway crosses the lane (GR 682922). **OS map:** Explorer 171 Chiltern Hills West.

How to get there

Option A: For the whole walk or Watlington Hill only walk:
From the A40, head north-west out of Stokenchurch and turn left, just past the huge concrete telecommunications tower, signposted to Christmas Common. After about 3.25 miles / 5 km (just before the village of Christmas Common)

turn right along Hill Road. The car park is on your left after 450 m. Postcode OX49 5HS.

Option B: For the Swyncombe and Cookley Green loop only:
From Watlington, head south-west on the B4009 towards Britwell Salome. At the crossroads in the centre of Britwell Salome, between Red Lion Farm and the Red Lion pub, turn left signposted towards Britwell Hill. After about 1 mile / 1.5 km (before the climb back up Britwell Hill) the lane crosses the Ridgeway (black signpost on the left) where there is some parking along the verges. Start the walk from Point 6. Nearest postcode OX49 5LQ.

Nearest refreshments

The Red Lion (☎ 01491 613140) at Britwell Salome is a stylish little village pub with a cottage garden. It has a good selection of real ales and serves fresh home-cooked pub classics with the emphasis on seasonal fresh ingredients. Postcode OX49 5LG www.redlionbritwellsalome.co.uk
A short drive from Cookley Green in Maidensgrove is the Five Horseshoes. Well worth a visit for its wonderful location on a ridge with outstanding views, this 16th-century pub serves real ales and traditional English dishes with a modern twist. Closed on Mondays. www.thefivehorseshoes.co.uk (☎ 01491 641282)
The Fox and Hounds (☎ 01491 612599) at Christmas Common welcomes walkers and dogs alike. It has a garden and boasts a selection of real ales and serves modern pub food made with local ingredients. Postcode OX49 5HL www.topfoxpub.co.uk

The Walk

1. From the car park at **Watlington Hill**, stand facing the exit to **Hill Road** and take the track on the left, by two large noticeboards. Follow the track through the trees and straight on over the track at the **National Trust Watlington Hill** sign. Go through the wooden gate and you'll soon be out on the open grassland at the top of **Watlington Hill**. Follow the grassy track straight ahead, past the black marker post. It later bears right heading downhill. Keep going, with **Watlington** in front of you, soon heading more steeply downhill, to the gate in the corner near the bottom.

2. Go through the gate and follow the track down to **Hill Road**. At the road keep left for around 15 m where you'll then turn left down a well-made wide track – the **Ridgeway**, with a restricted access sign for vehicles.

3. After about 180 m you'll see a gate in the hedgerow on your left. If you are doing the **Watlington Hill** only walk: follow the walk from Point 13. If you

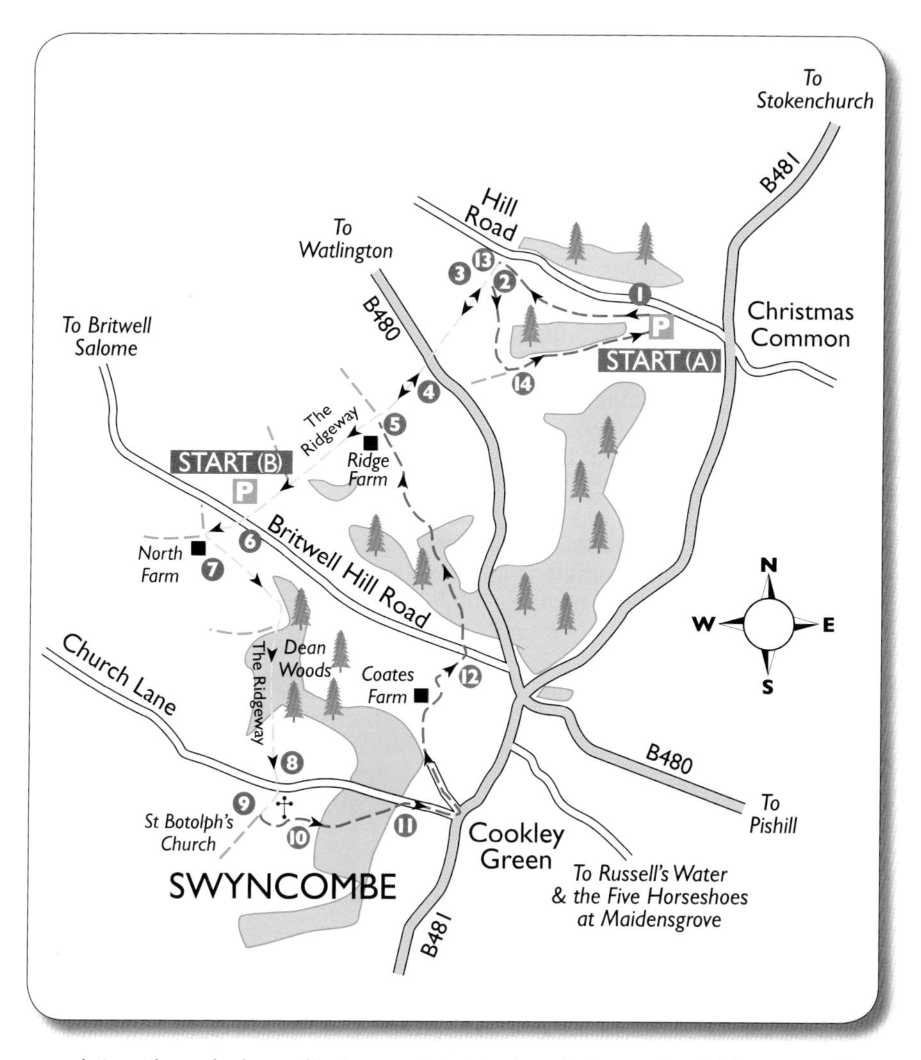

are doing the whole walk: keep straight ahead along the **Ridgeway**. You may want to put your dog on a lead as after a further 700 metres the track emerges at a fairly busy road (B480).

4 Cross the road and follow the black **Ridgeway** signpost ahead. The Ridgeway here is a narrow lane with the occasional car. If you prefer, you can take the permissive footpath (indicated on the **Copas Farm** sign) through the field (by the gate on your left), which runs alongside the Ridgeway.

5. You'll emerge from the permissive footpath by a metal farm gate at an intersection of tracks with a black signpost. With the signpost behind you, follow the sign for the Ridgeway down the track ahead (also signposted to **Ridge Farm** which you'll soon pass on your left). This section can be quite muddy and there is an alternative footpath on raised ground on the left, running alongside the Ridgeway. After a further 1,100 m you'll arrive at a small lane (**Britwell Hill Road**).

6. Cross the lane and continue straight ahead. If you are doing the **Swyncombe & Cookley Green loop only**, park and start the walk here. With the black signpost for the Ridgeway behind you and the lane rising up to **Britwell Hill** on your left, follow the sign ahead for the Ridgeway down the track, past the noticeboard with the map. After around 300 m the track divides.

7. At the marker post, turn left towards the farm buildings (still on the Ridgeway) and then bear left again to follow the path ahead (with the barns of **North Farm** on your right). At the next marker post keep straight ahead, following the path as it starts to climb uphill. Keep going uphill to **Dean Wood**. At the top of the hill the path emerges from the woods. Keep going ahead on the Ridgeway as it now heads back downhill alongside the fields, and straight on down into the valley and then back up the other side.

8. Go through the gate at the top of the hill and cross **Church Lane**, following the black signpost ahead for the Ridgeway. The road bears right, passing the ancient **church of St Botolph** on your left.

9. Go through the side gate on your left, into the churchyard (by the black

painted parish noticeboard). Then take the path out of the churchyard through the yew hedge (opposite the church porch) and out through the gate, with **Home Farm** in front of you. Then turn left and after about 20 m bear right through the trees then, keeping left at the next fork, arrive at a driveway by the telegraph pole. Cross the driveway and take the narrow path alongside the wooden fence opposite.

10 After about 45 m, at the gate, pop your dog on a lead as there could be sheep in the next field. Then go through the gate and follow the grassy track ahead, uphill towards the woodland in front of you. Go through the gate into the woods and follow the white painted arrows straight ahead on the main path. Keep going to the edge of the woods, following the marker posts straight on.

11 At **Church Lane** turn right, following the **Chiltern Way** signpost, and walk for about 300 m to **Cookley Green**. At the junction of roads, turn left, along Coates Lane, keeping the cricket pavilion on your left, and pass a row of cottages on your right. After about 250 m the road becomes a track as it enters woodland. Keep going straight ahead past **Coates Farm** (on your left).

12 Cross **Britwell Hill Road** at the signpost and take the bridleway ahead, signposted to **Britwell Autos** and **Woods Farm**. At **Woods Farm** follow the marked bridleway and then keep on the main path ahead, following the white arrows through the trees on the sunken bridleway, ignoring any paths off. It descends gradually, eventually passing **Dame Alice Farm** on your left, where the track becomes a gravel lane, emerging shortly after at the intersection of paths at Point 5. If you parked at Point 6, turn left here back to your starting point. If you parked on top of **Watlington Hill**, turn right and re-trace your steps back along the permissive footpath through the field on your right and then on to the gate at Point 13.

13 Go through the gate in the hedgerow (with the DEFRA arrow and conservation walk maps on the gatepost). This route offers a more gradual, gentle climb back up to the car park at the top of **Watlington Hill**. Follow the wide track that bears right across the middle of the field. At the fenced hedgerows, stay on the grassy path as it bears right and downhill across the next field to the metal farm gate in the corner.

14 Go through the gate and then almost immediately go left through the wooden gate on your left. This path heads gradually uphill through the trees. Go through the next gate (by the National Trust **Watlington Hill** sign) and keep straight ahead, climbing gradually back uphill, ignoring any paths off, eventually through two more gates and back to the car park at the top of the hill.

14

Crowell

The Talking Trail at Aston Rowant Nature Reserve.

This walk along the edge of a high Chiltern escarpment has stunning views across the surrounding landscape. Dogs will enjoy exploring the variety of terrain, whilst their humans can appreciate the vistas afforded by the diverse landscape along the way. The Ridgeway section follows the (now dismantled) railway between Princes Risborough and Watlington, along a wide tree-lined track. It then leaves the Ridgeway for a loop through the delightful chalk grasslands of the Aston Rowant Nature Reserve, taking in part of the 'Talking Trail' (eye-catching wooden sculptures with wind-up listening posts where you can hear a short audio clip). It then returns via National Trust ancient beech woodland (following a section of the original London to Oxford turnpike), before linking back up with the Ridgeway trail.

Dog factors

Distance: 7 miles / 11.5 km.
Road Walking: 100 m at point 10.
Livestock: None, though pheasants are present during shooting season (Nov-Jan). Deer in Aston Wood from point 9 (there is a road down the escarpment so you may wish to leash your dog here if it chases deer).
Stiles: None.
Nearest vets: Hall Place Veterinary Centre, 1A Dodds Corner, New Road, Stokenchurch HP14 3RZ ☎ 01494 485855.

Terrain

The Ridgeway section is fairly level, then there is a moderately long ascent, fairly steep in sections, through the Aston Rowant Nature Reserve and a corresponding descent through woodland back to the Ridgeway. The woodland paths are quite muddy in winter and after prolonged wet weather.

Where to park

If you plan to visit the Shepherd's Crook pub at Crowell there is limited parking by the pub (GR 744997). Otherwise, park roadside. There is parking for several cars where the Ridgeway crosses Kingston Hill at Point 3 (GR 742986). **OS map:** Explorer 171 Chiltern Hills West.

How to get there

From Junction 6 of the M40 take the B4009 signed to Chinnor. After just over 2 miles (3.5 km) in the hamlet of Crowell, turn right when you see the church and pub sign on your right. There are a few places to park on the verge here or if you are visiting the pub, it has a small car park. Postcode OX39 4RR.

Nearest refreshments

The Shepherd's Crook (☎ 01844 355266) at Crowell serves a variety of ales from independent breweries and traditional fresh, seasonal food using local ingredients. Postcode: OX39 4RR www.the-shepherds-crook.co.uk

The Walk

1. From the Shepherd's Crook, continue down the lane, with the pub on your right, past the cottages and straight on across the open fields. At the edge of the field, at the marker post, keep straight ahead.

2. At the end of the next field, at the black signpost at the intersection of tracks, turn right along the **Ridgeway** (public bridleway). After about 1,000 m the Ridgeway crosses a lane (**Kingston Hill**).

3. Keep straight ahead here, following the Ridgeway for a further 1.5 km.

4. With your dog on a lead, approach the busy A40 road. Cross over and go straight on, following the black Ridgeway signpost. Head up the track and shortly after, at the noticeboard for **Aston Rowant Nature Reserve**, keep straight ahead, still on the Ridgeway. You'll start to hear the hum of the M40 and the track bears left. Keep going at the next black Ridgeway signpost and then, as the M40 comes into view ahead, you'll see another marker post, a map and a noticeboard.

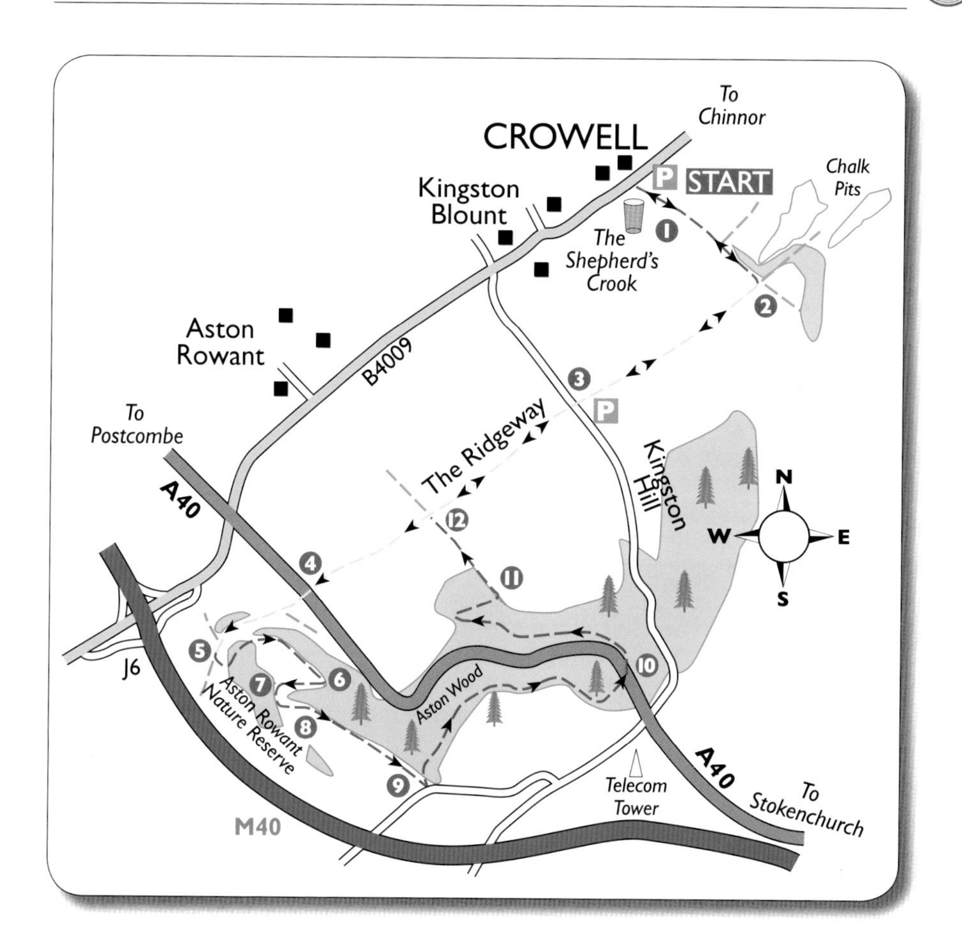

5 Turn left here through the metal gate into the **Aston Rowant Nature Reserve**, and then almost immediately, go through the double wooden gate to the left of the nature reserve map. Head uphill along the grassy path to the next marker post (about 60 m on). Bear left here following the dark green arrow for the **Aston Rowant Discovery Trail** (**ARDT**). The path bears right, around the side of the hill with views off to your left. Keep going on this path, through the metal gate, still following the green arrows. Head uphill, ignoring any side paths, through another metal gate and on to where the path divides at a marker post.

6. At the marker post, the light green Sculpture Trail arrow heads straight on but you'll turn right, following the dark green arrow uphill through the trees. Go through the metal gate at the top of the hill where you'll see a wooden sculpture on your left. Keep straight on here for about 60 m, with the fence (and views) on your right.

7. At the next wooden sculpture and marker post, turn left, following the green ARDT arrows. A short distance on (approx. 20 m) the path forks – take the left-hand fork, again following the green arrow on the marker post. The grasslands here are covered with small green hillocks, which are anthills made by yellow meadow ants. Some of the anthills are believed to be up to 100 years old! Keep straight on towards a gate by the trees.

8. Go through the wooden gate into the woods and follow the path ahead along the top edge of the woodland (with open fields on your right). You'll now follow this woodland path straight ahead for around 700 m, past another 'talking' sculpture, ignoring any paths off. Eventually you'll meet a small lane by an old green signpost.

9. At the lane turn sharp left along the marked footpath, following the white arrow painted on the tree and passing a seating area on your right. Keep going into the woods, following the white arrows as the path bears right. You'll soon see an **Aston Woods** National Trust sign. Keep straight ahead, ignoring any paths off and following the white arrows through the trees, along the edge of the woods, for around 1,500 m. Eventually, the path bears left and you'll arrive at a busy road (A40).

10. Dogs on leads here for the road. Go through the gate and turn left (cross the road where there is a better path) and walk for about 100 m. As the road bears left, re-enter the woods on your right, at the **Aston Wood** National Trust sign. The wide track goes downhill and follows the route of the old London to Oxford Turnpike. About half way down the hill the track divides at a 'No Riding' sign. Keep straight on here (now ignoring the white arrow), past the 'No Riding' sign (which also has a green arrow). This path descends gradually and at the bottom of the hill, by the marker post and a house, the track takes a sharp right, and after about 150 m meets a track.

11. Turn left along the track by the National Trust **Juniper Bank** sign and follow it (and the white arrows again) through the woods, to emerge onto a wide grassy rutted track. Keep straight ahead to the tree-line and a black sign post.

12. Turn right along the **Ridgeway** and re-trace your steps to your starting point.

Bledlow and Lodge Hill

This scenic walk starts from the Lions at Bledlow, a pub in a lovely village on the edge of the Chilterns. There are wonderful views over the Vale of Aylesbury for the first half of the walk and the route soon picks up the Ridgeway as it crosses undulating farmland to Lodge Hill, an elevated Site of Special Scientific Interest (SSSI). Its chalk grassland and scrub supports a variety of wildlife, including badger, deer, rabbit and many butterflies – providing plenty of sensory doggy delights! The walk returns via the Chiltern Way through the valley, passing several beautiful cottages, farms and converted barns that are characteristic of the area.

Terrain

This is a fairly open walk with a mixture of footpaths and tracks through scattered woodland, across farmland and over chalk grassland. One moderate and one fairly steep ascent and corresponding descent.

Where to park

If you are visiting the Lions of Bledlow pub, it has a large car park (behind the pub, about 40 m down the track to the right of the pub), otherwise park along the verges of Church End (GR 776021). **OS map:** Explorer 171 Chiltern Hills West.

How to get there

Turn off the B4009 between Chinnor and Princes Risborough into West Lane, with the brown signpost to the Lions of Bledlow pub. You'll come to a grassy triangular village green with the pub in front of you. Postcode HP27 9PE.

Nearest refreshments

The Lions of Bledlow (☎ 01844 343345) is a 16th-century free house that serves a good range of real ales and traditional pub food. Postcode HP27 9PE www.thelionsofbledlow.co.uk

Dog factors

Distance: 5 miles / 7.8 km
Road Walking: 500 m in Saunderton and 650 m through Bledlow to return to the pub.
Livestock: Sheep grazing in some fields.
Stiles: 3 – with passing places, suitable for all but the largest dogs.
Nearest Vets: Sprinz & Nash, Wellington House Veterinary Surgery, Aylesbury Road, Princes Risborough, HP27 0JP ☎ 01844 345655.

The Walk

1. From the **Lions of Bledlow** pub, take the track that runs alongside the pub with the green signpost indicating 'Bridleway to Ridgeway'. After about

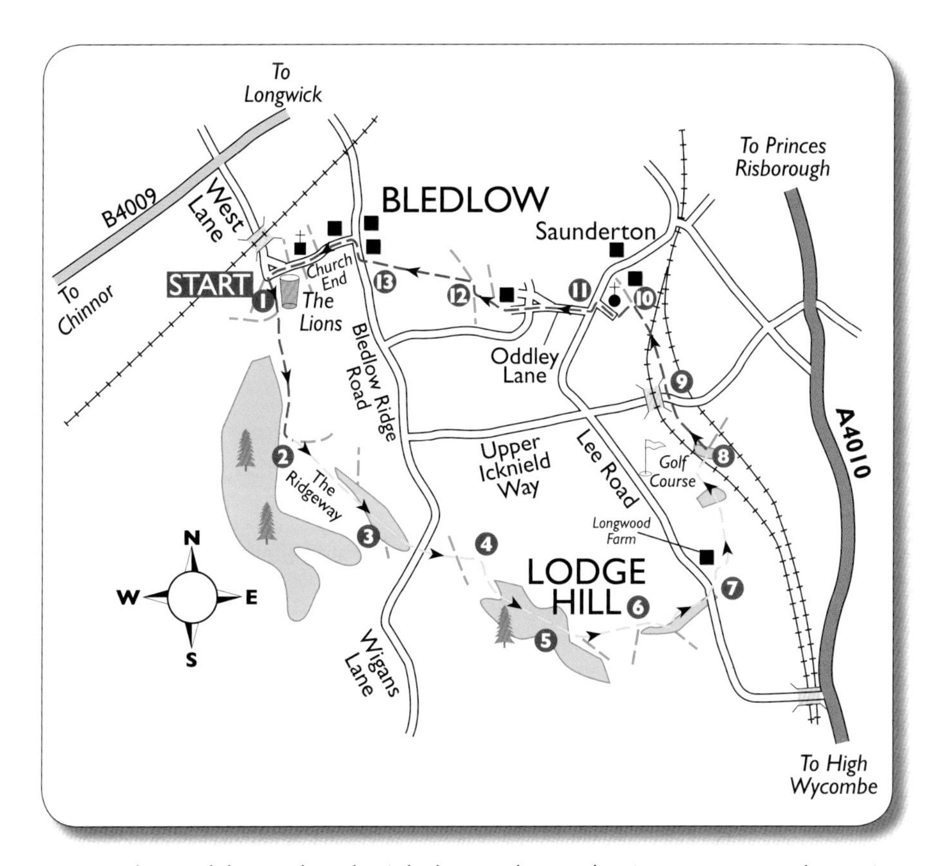

225 m, the track bears sharply right by a pylon and a signpost. Leave the main track here and follow the footpath straight ahead (indicated as 'Bridleway to Ridgeway West'), past the pylon on your right, leading uphill through the trees. Keep going on a long slow ascent for around 700 m.

2 At the top of the hill, you'll meet the **Ridgeway** at a black signpost. Turn left here and after about only 20 m, at the next black signpost, leave the track and turn right, following the Ridgeway footpath sign through the gate into the field (where sheep may be grazing). Now head across the field, bearing slightly left. After about 200 m the path meets a tree-line. Keep going ahead with the tree-line on your left, following the black marker posts for the Ridgeway.

3 In the corner of the field, go through the gate and turn right – then keep straight ahead on the Ridgeway footpath. After about 300 m you'll reach a road at a gate. You may need your dog on a lead as you cross the road and take the path through the next gate opposite, still following the black signposts for the **Ridgeway**. Keep going diagonally across the corner of the field, through the next gate in the hedgerow and then straight ahead again to the marker post in the middle of the field, at the intersection of tracks. Keep straight on to the next gate in the hedgerow at the base of **Lodge Hill**.

4 Go through the gate and turn right, following the path ahead. Keep going straight on at the black marker post, as the path then enters the woodland and heads uphill. At the top the path emerges from the trees onto the chalky grassland of **Lodge Hill**. Keep following the path, and black marker posts, straight ahead.

5 At a wooden gate the path re-enters some woodland. Keep straight on here, ignoring any paths off and following the black marker posts. The path soon bears slightly left and descends more steeply.

6 Go through the gate near the bottom of the hill, with the black signpost, and keep straight ahead on the **Ridgeway Bridleway** path. Keep going at the next marker post as the path runs along the right-hand edge of a field. Follow the path (hedgerow on your right) to the black signpost. The path bears left here – signposted Ridgeway Bridleway. Keep going (hedgerow still on your right), under the power lines and on to the road.

7 Cross the road and follow the Ridgeway ahead down the track between the two wooden fences. At the gated entrance to **Longwood Farm**, take the footpath on the right that runs alongside the high wooden fence. Then keep

ahead on a long grassy path between trees bordering fields on each side. At the end of the path, in the trees, go through the next gate and shortly after, at the marker post (on the old gatepost) take the path on your right, following the yellow arrow and acorn symbol. You'll soon notice that the path crosses a golf course, so dogs on leads. Follow the black marker posts and pass the clubhouse away to your left. The path then bears right to a railway line crossing so dogs on leads now.

8 Cross carefully over the railway line (at the Stop, Look & Listen gated crossing), and then keep straight on through a copse. Go through the next gate and then, at the black signpost in the field, turn left on the footpath indicated (leaving the Ridgeway). Head across the field and at the house, go over the stile, and pass the house on your right, then down the driveway and past the tennis court on your left, to the road.

9 Cross the road and take the path opposite. Now follow the path straight ahead for about 420 m to a stile and then, with your dog on a lead, up some steps to another Stop, Look & Listen railway crossing. Cross carefully and go down the steps on the other side, then ahead on the path. After about 200 m, look out for a marker post on your left in the hedgerow.

10 Turn left at the marker post, passing under the power lines and soon crossing a stream to a churchyard. Cross the churchyard and keep going on the path to the signpost by the house. Turn right here (dogs on leads for some road walking) and follow **Church Lane** for 75 m, past the pond, to the road. Now turn left along the road for 60 m to the grassy triangle and signpost.

11 At the junction turn right. Walk along **Oddley Lane** for about 350 m where it bears sharply left. You'll see a private track ahead (to the farm) and just to the left of it, by the telegraph pole, go through the wooden gate, to follow the path ahead along the right-hand edge of the field, parallel to the driveway. Just past the farmhouse, the track bears right, but keep straight ahead at the marker post, following the yellow arrow, on the grassy track towards the tree-line.

12 Go over the stile at the edge of the field and then turn right at the junction of tracks. Then, after just 45 m, at the marker post, turn left, following the blue bridleway arrow, heading diagonally across the field.

13 In the corner of the field pop your dog on the lead for the road and go through the gate. Turn right and walk for about 150 m. Just after the 30 mph sign, at the white signpost, turn left along **Church End** and follow this village road back to your parking place.

Whiteleaf Hill and Pulpit Hill

This wonderful walk starts with the breathtaking views across the Vale of Aylesbury from the top of Whiteleaf Hill. Much of the walk follows the celebrated Ridgeway and Icknield Way footpaths, passing through the Pulpit Hill Nature Reserve, ancient ash and beech woodland and past the

Plough at Lower Cadsden, a dog-friendly traditional English pub. This is idyllic English countryside at its best! Dogs can run free most of the way, enjoying the sights, sounds and smells of the rich and varied landscape. The chalk downland of the nature reserve is home to several species of wild flower, orchid and butterfly and Pulpit Hill is the site of an Iron Age fort, where the ditches and earthworks are still evident.

Dog factors

Distance: 3 miles / 5 km.
Road walking: 125 m past the Plough at Lower Cadsden.
Livestock: Yes, livestock may be present in the nature reserve.
Stiles: None.
Nearest vets: Sprinz & Nash, Wellington House Veterinary Surgery, Aylesbury Road, Princes Risborough HP27 0JP. ☎ 01844 345655.

Terrain

There is one fairly steep ascent up to Pulpit Hill, from the nature reserve and another more gradual ascent back up to Whiteleaf towards the end of the walk. The chalk grasslands drain well and stay firm underfoot in all but the wettest weather, however the many woodland bridleways get quite muddy after rain and in winter.

Where to park

There is a free car park and picnic area near the top of Whiteleaf Hill (GR 823036). **OS map:** Explorer 181 Chiltern Hills North.

How to get there

Turn off the A4010 at Monks Risborough (just north of Princes Risborough) at Peter's Lane (alongside the school) signposted to Hampden, Whiteleaf and Whiteleaf Cross. At the top of the long steep hill, the car park will be found on your left-hand side marked by a brown tourist signpost for Whiteleaf Cross and Hill. Postcode HP27 0RP.

Nearest refreshments

Whiteleaf Hill is a perfect place for a picnic on a warm day and there are a few picnic tables at the car park area. The Plough (☎ 01844 343302) at Lower Cadsden is a traditional English pub that serves hearty home-cooked food. The Ridgeway runs right past the pub and dogs are welcome in the garden. Postcode HP27 0NB www.theplough.pub

The Walk

1. Head to the far end of the car park by the noticeboard. Continue on for about 75 m to the main track. Turn right here and follow the well-made track of the **Ridgeway** straight ahead. After about 300 m go through the wooden gate and onto the grassy hilltop of **Whiteleaf Hill**.

2. At the black signpost on top of the hill, turn right and follow the **Ridgeway** footpath into the woods. Go through the metal gate and follow the trail, gradually downhill. It then bears left and heads more steeply downhill. Further down, at the intersection of paths with the signpost, stay straight ahead and downhill on the Ridgeway footpath. Go through the metal gate at the bottom of the hill to the pub car park.

3. Turn left, following the track past the pub - dogs on leads here for the road ahead. Keep straight ahead when it joins the road, and after about 15 m, take the footpath on the opposite side of the road, through the post and rail fence

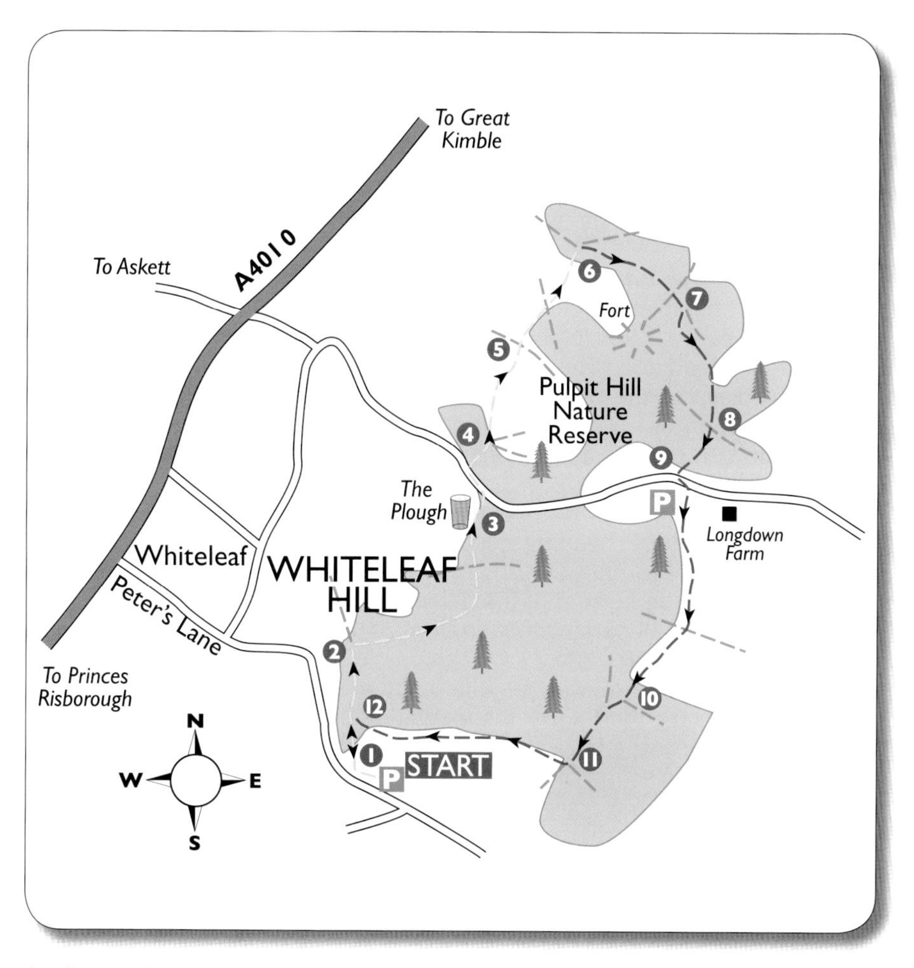

(with a 'red route' sign on the post). Follow the path to a wooden gate (you'll see another gate a few metres to your left).

4 Go through the gate and turn left, then follow the Ridgeway through the nature reserve.

5 Go through the wooden gate in front of you at the edge of the reserve and then straight on past the signpost, and through the metal gate, following

the Ridgeway. Keep straight on at the next intersection of paths, which soon heads steeply uphill, and up some rough steps to a wooden gate. Go through the gate and continue up the steps.

6 At the signpost at the top, turn right, (signposted Ridgeway) and then keep straight ahead on the path. Near the top of the hill keep straight on at the intersection of paths (at the footpath marker post with the blue arrow).

7 About 45 m further on, you'll need to leave the main track. Look out for and take a small unmarked, slightly raised path on your right - it's easy to miss. You'll soon see a section of broken down barbed wire fence on your left. Stay straight ahead and soon after, just as it looks like this path will rejoin the main track, keep to the right, still going straight ahead. Follow the path on through a section of mainly pine woodland, the path eventually bears right and downhill, to emerge at an intersection of paths and a signpost to **Pulpit Hill Fort**.

8 Go straight across here, heading steeply downhill (towards the bottom of the hill, you may want to put your dog on a lead as you will soon be crossing a country road). At the bottom of the hill you re-join the Ridgeway again, by a signpost, with a small parking area in front of you.

9 Turn left along the bridleway, parallel to the road. After about 100 m the bridleway meets the road. Cross the road and take the bridleway opposite by the signpost. Follow the track slightly downhill through the trees. After about 450 m, at the intersection of paths, go straight on.

10 Then, about 330 m further on, you'll see a marker post with a footpath to your left. Bear right here, following the blue public bridleway sign downhill. After about 20 m the path meets a main track at another marker post, turn left here following the blue arrow. Now keep straight ahead, heading uphill (ignoring any paths off) for about another 300 m.

11 At the top of the hill, with a field in front of you, turn right along the Icknield Way. Keep straight on, parallel to the field, ignoring any paths off.

12 At the end of the field, the path meets a well-made track (Ridgeway) by a black signpost. Turn left and follow it back to the start.

Coombe Hill and Chequers

Chequers Court.

This walk, through a variety of beautiful Chiltern grassy chalk downland, woodland and fields, also enjoys some stunning views across the Vale of Aylesbury from two vantage points, Coombe Hill (the highest viewpoint in the Chilterns) and the iconic grassy mound of Beacon Hill. Around half the route follows the Ridgeway trail, which forms a loop around Chequers, the Prime Minister's country house retreat, winding through the largest native box tree woodland in England and passing the delightful church in the village of Ellesborough. Coombe Hill is a great spot to enjoy a picnic on a warm day by the monument, which is dedicated to the men from Buckinghamshire who gave their lives in the Boer War – and there's plenty of space for dogs to chase a ball and run free.

Terrain

The grassy chalk downlands of Coombe Hill and Beacon Hill remain generally firm underfoot, however the field and woodland sections of the walk will be muddy in winter and after prolonged rain. There is one very steep descent from Coombe Hill and two shortish, but fairly demanding ascents.

Where to park

There is a good car park off Lodge Hill with easy access to Coombe Hill (GR 852062). **OS map:** Explorer 181 Chiltern Hills North.

How to get there

From Princes Risborough, head north on the A4010, passing through Monks Risborough, Askett and Great Kimble. Shortly after Great Kimble turn right, signposted to Butlers Cross and Ellesborough. After 1.25 miles / 2 km, turn right in Butlers Cross (Missenden Road). About 0.8 miles / 1.5 km turn left into Lodge Hill. The car park is almost a mile up the hill on a sharp right-hand bend. Postcode HP17 0UR.

Nearest refreshments

The Plough (☎ 01844 343302) at Lower Cadsden is a traditional English pub that serves hearty home-cooked food. Dogs are welcome in the garden. Postcode HP27 0NB www.theplough.pub
The Russell Arms (☎ 01296 624 411) at Butlers Cross is a traditional coaching inn, serving a range of cask ales and modern freshly cooked food using local produce. Postcode: HP17 0TS www.therussellarms.co.uk

Dog factors

Distance: 4.5 miles / 7 km.
Road walking: 100 m at Point 4 and 30 m in Ellesborough
Livestock: Cattle are likely to be grazing on Coombe Hill but keep a watchful eye for livestock that may be present at other points on the walk, depending on the time of year.
Stiles: None.
Nearest vets: Sprinz & Nash, Wellington House Veterinary Surgery, Aylesbury Road, Princes Risborough, HP27 0JP.

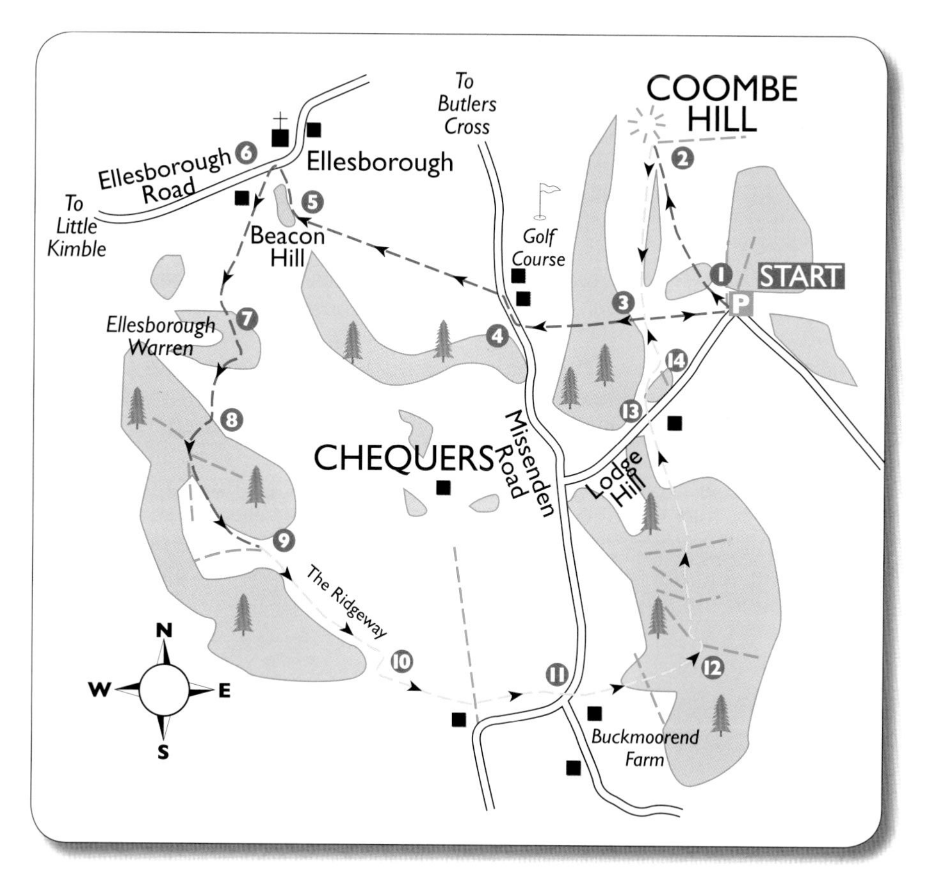

The Walk

1 From the car park on **Lodge Hill**, head back towards the road and go through the gate on your right (just by the road). Now go straight ahead on the wide grassy track. There will be cattle grazing here. At the stand of trees, keep going and the path bears right as it emerges onto the chalky downs of **Coombe Hill**. You'll see the **Boer War Memorial** up ahead of you – keep going till you reach it.

2 At the monument, after enjoying the views, turn back round to face the way you came and you'll see a roughly parallel path, to the right of the line of trees and shrubs, slightly down the hillside, by a marker post. Follow this path (**Ridgeway**) straight ahead with the escarpment dropping away to your right.

Keep going ahead for about 550 metres until the path meets a metal gate at the edge of the woods in front of you.

3. Turn right, just before the metal gate and the path will soon head very steeply downhill with a fence on your left side. At the bottom, by the National Trust Coombe Hill sign, go straight ahead through the gate and down the track, past a golf course on your right, to a road.

4. Cross the road and turn right. After about 100 metres, at the footpath signpost, turn left and head diagonally across the middle of the field on the path.

5. In the opposite corner of the field, the path narrows through the trees and emerges by a green signpost at a track. Turn right along the track, which meets the road after about 150 metres by **Ellesborough church**.

6. Turn left here, along the roadside footpath for about 30 metres, and at the footpath sign, turn left through the gate into the field. Now head across the field towards the grassy mound of **Beacon Hill**. Go through the next gate, in the tree-line, and the follow the path ahead as it bears slightly right – heading uphill, around the right-hand side of Beacon Hill.

Coombe Hill Monument.

7 Go through the gate at the woodland. The narrow path winds through **Ellesborough Warren** and shortly climbs up a series of rough steps. At the top, go through the gate, and across the field ahead.

8 Go through the next gate, re-entering the woodland. The path then bears left, and crosses a track (leading to private woodland). Go through the next gate ahead of you, and keep straight ahead, following the path along the tree-line, with the fence on your left.

9 In the corner of the field go through the gate, following the Ridgeway track, bound by a fence on your left and woodland on your right. You'll soon get a good view of **Chequers** across the field on your left.

10 The path eventually bears right near the black marker post, and 50 m further on, at the **Ridgeway** signpost, turn left through the gate. Follow the footpath across the field. At the edge of the field, by the Chequers gatehouses, go straight through the next 3 gates and follow the path ahead for about 280 m to a road.

11 Cross the road by the sign for **Buckmoorend Farm Shop** to the black Ridgeway signpost. Now follow the Ridgeway bridleway ahead, uphill, past the farm on your right, into the woodland. Keep following the black marker posts, soon crossing over the **South Bucks Way** (at the next signpost) to the top of the hill.

12 At the black signpost at the top of the hill turn left (Ridgeway). The path forks immediately – take the upper, right-hand fork that runs on the level through the trees. The Ridgeway now follows a series of black marker posts and signposts. Keep following the Ridgeway signs through the woods for around 750 m. Eventually the path runs alongside a wooden fence on your left and you'll see a barn in a field on your right. Soon after, you'll emerge by a road and a black signpost.

13 Almost directly opposite you, across the road, take the unmarked path into the woods (it saves you walking along the road). The path winds through the woods and shortly after some huge trees with multiple trunks (one with a large bough that swoops over the path) it bears sharp right to a marker post where it re-joins the Ridgeway.

14 Turn left at this marker post and follow the path to a metal gate and a signpost (at Point 3). Go through the gate and turn sharp right, following the path back to the car park.

18

Swan Bottom and Hale Wood

Starting in the pretty rural hamlet of Swan Bottom, this walk meanders through woods and farmland to pick up the Ridgeway trail as it winds for just over a mile along a wooded Chiltern ridge, through Hale Wood and Barn Wood (the southernmost reaches of Wendover Woods). It's a lovely stroll along this ancient track under the shady trees and there's plenty to keep your dog busy along the way. It passes remote farmhouses and returns via the hamlet of Lee Gate, with the 16th-century Old Swan pub making a fine place to finish the walk.

Dog factors

Distance: 4.5 miles / 7 km.
Road walking: 45 m at Lee Gate.
Livestock: Possible livestock in the fields and after Kings Ash Farm
Stiles: 4: The first stile at Point 7 is not particularly dog friendly – there is a hole to the right and then enough room (about 12 inches under the fence) for a large dog to scrabble under. The stile between Points 9 & 10 is similar. The two other stiles are suitable for all but the largest of dogs.
Nearest vets: Wendover Heights Veterinary Centre, Tring Road, Halton HP22 5PN ☎ 01296 623439.

Terrain

Open farmland and woodland make up the majority of this walk. There is one long but gradual ascent at the end of the Ridgeway coming out of Barn Wood, but otherwise the walk is mostly level.

Where to park

Park near the Old Swan pub at Swan Bottom (GR 902055). **OS map:** Explorer 181 Chiltern Hills North.

How to get there

From the A413, about a mile south of Wendover (heading south to Great Missenden) just after the petrol station, turn left along Rocky Lane, signposted to Kings Ash and The Lee. Follow this road for about 2 miles / 3 km and at the crossroads, in the hamlet of Swan Bottom, turn left, signposted to St Leonards. The Old Swan pub is on the left. Postcode HP16 9NU.

Nearest refreshments

The Old Swan pub (☎ 01494 837239) in Swan Bottom has a pretty beer garden and a cosy bar with a roaring fire in the winter. It serves home-cooked pub classics using fresh local ingredients. Postcode: HP16 9NU www.theoldswanpub.co.uk

The Walk

1. Take the track past the pub on your right and a row of cottages on your left. The track enters **Lordling Wood** and then divides – take the right fork – and

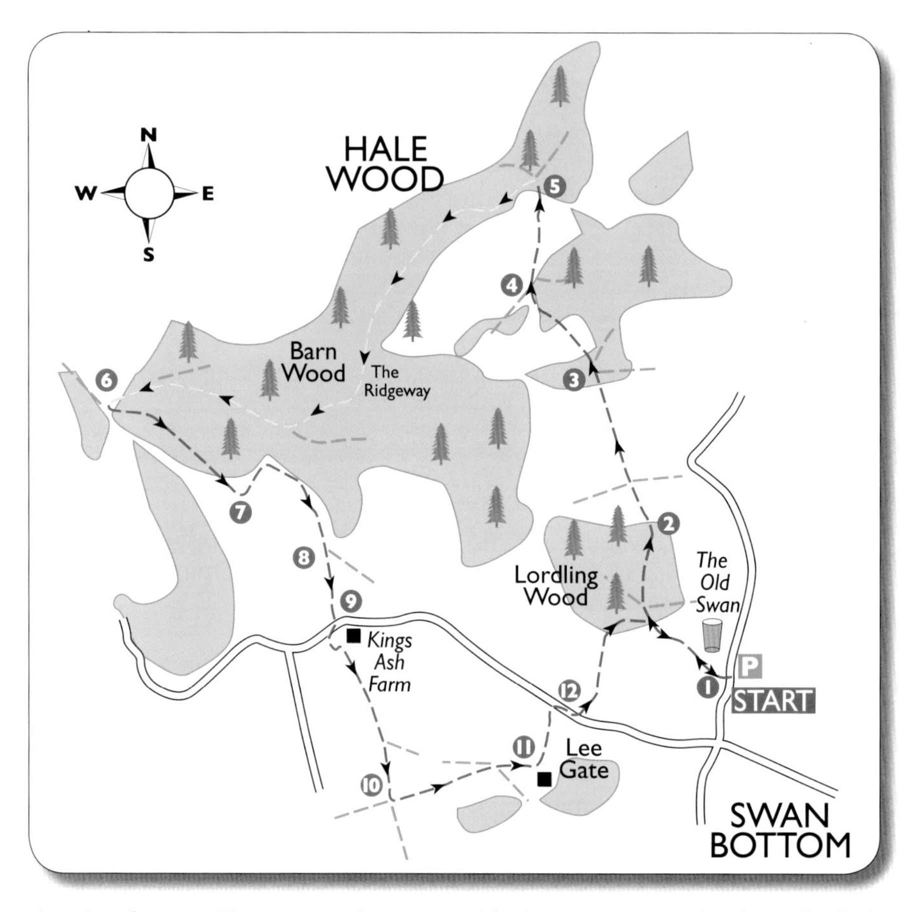

shortly after you'll see a marker post with three arrows. Take the right fork again here (not the sharp right footpath) through the woods.

2 The path becomes a little indistinct as it reaches the edge of the woodland but keep straight ahead and you'll see a marker post by the field in front of you. The path now bears left across the middle of the field. At the break in the hedgerow keep straight ahead across the middle of the next field, heading towards the woodland.

3 At the marker post by the woodland, go straight ahead, then pass through the fence about 15 m further on, following the yellow arrow ahead. The path shortly leaves the woods again – follow the path across the field ahead, to the line of trees in front of you. At the trees, the path bears left and then right, around the right-hand edge of the field and then into a corner of the woodland.

4 Keep straight on here, towards the next field in front of you, ignoring any paths off. Take the path ahead, which cuts off the corner of the field to your right, to a marker post in front of you. Keep straight ahead, along the edge of the field, towards an old brick wall that is falling down in places.

5 Go through the notch cut in the brick wall by the metal farm gate to the courtyard of the house on your right. Follow the path ahead, slightly downhill through the trees into **Hale Wood**. After about 75 m you'll see a black signpost for the **Ridgeway**. Turn left here and follow the well-made track for just over a mile. Ignore any paths off and keep straight ahead. Eventually, the Ridgeway path reaches the bottom of a hill, running alongside a fence on your right and then passing a Ridgeway noticeboard.

6 Shortly after you'll arrive at an intersection of tracks and a black Ridgeway signpost. Turn left following the sign for **Chiltern Link & Bridleway**. Then almost immediately, the path forks – take the left fork that leads uphill through the trees. The two paths run parallel for about 75 m then the lower one turns sharply right. Keep straight on heading uphill.

7 At the top of the hill the path emerges from the woods. Go through the gate and keep straight ahead passing the barns on your left and the farmhouse on your right. At the driveway go over the stile in front of you. You are heading for a stile at the edge of the woods (diagonally across the field to your right) but the pathway runs around the edge of the field, so turn left once over the stile and follow the trees and hedge along on your left, round to the end of the tree-line.

8 Go over the stile and take the grassy track straight ahead along the hedgerow on your right, towards the houses in front of you.

9 At the gate, pop your dog on the lead and go straight ahead, through a garden with chickens in, to a road. Cross over and take the track opposite, signposted Chiltern Link and Kings Ash Barn. The driveway bears left and just here, on your right, is a gate. Go through the gate and cross the track, going over the stile. Then, go through the next gate and across the field, bearing right to its opposite corner. Go over the stile and straight ahead with the hedgerow on your left. After about 150 m you'll notice a gap in the hedgerow on your left with a broken down stile – ignore this and keep going ahead.

10 At the next gap in the hedgerow (about 170 m further on) turn left, taking the grassy track that runs through the middle of the field. You'll pass a telegraph pole on your left and see a marker post – go straight on here.

11 At the edge of the field (with the tumbledown barns in front of you), turn left through the gate and follow the path ahead past the farmhouse on your left. Keep going for another 100 metres until the track meets a country lane with an old pub sign for **Lee Gate** (the pub is now a house).

12 Turn right along the lane for about 45 m and then turn left along the track by the telegraph pole, signposted **Chiltern Way & Byway**. The track soon enters **Lordling Wood** and bears right and slightly downhill, shortly afterwards meeting the intersection of paths at Point 1. Turn right here and retrace your steps back to the Old Swan pub.

19

Pitstone Hill and The Ashridge Estate

This is a walk across a varied landscape that takes in the part of the Ridgeway trail that crosses Pitstone Hill, with its wonderful views and plenty of space for energetic dogs to run free. The scenic trail continues through the ancient National Trust woodland of Aldbury Nowers, passing gnarled trees through which there are lovely views over the valley. The return leg follows a delightful woodland trail through Moneybury Hill (past the remains of a Bronze Age burial barrow) and Pitstone Common. Commoners from Pitstone, Ivinghoe and Aldbury used to graze their animals on the land, however the area has reverted to woodland over the last 100 years as grazing has died out. Both are part of the National Trust's 5,000 acre Ashridge Estate.

Terrain

Open fields, chalk downlands and ancient woodland form the basis of this walk and make a nice mix of sheltered, shady trails and open fields and downs. There is one fairly steep ascent to Moneybury Hill (about half way round). Part of the walk skirts Stocks Golf Course.

Where to park

Park in the car park off the narrow lane (Stocks Road) that runs between the B488 at Ivinghoe and Aldbury village. The car park has a 1.7 m height restriction (GR 955150). **OS map:** Explorer 181 Chiltern Hills North.

How to get there

From Ivinghoe village, take the B488 towards Tring & Aylesbury. After 0.5 miles / 1 km the B488 makes a sharp right-hand bend. Turn off the B488 at the bend onto the small lane with the sign forbidding trucks over 7.5t (Stocks Road). The car park is on the right. Postcode HP23 5RX.

Nearest refreshments

There are two pubs in the nearby picturesque village of Aldbury. The Greyhound Inn (☎ 01442 851228) is a small family-run country hotel and inn that takes pride in serving top quality fresh food. It has a small courtyard garden and benches out front. Dogs are allowed in the bar. Postcode: HP23 5RT www.greyhoundaldbury.co.uk

The Valiant Trooper (☎ 01442 851203) is a dog-friendly country pub serving a variety of real ales and British pub food. It has a garden and was a 2015 winner of the Walkers' & Cyclists' Pub Award. Postcode: HP23 5RW www.valianttrooper.co.uk

The Brownlow Café is a short detour from the route at Moneybury Hill www.brownlowcafe.co.uk

Dog factors

Distance: 4.5 miles / 7.5 km.
Road walking: None.
Livestock: Yes, livestock may be present on Pitstone Hill and towards the end of the walk from Point 15.
Stiles: None.
Nearest vets: Springwell Vets, 98 Western Road, Tring HP23 4BJ ☎ 01442 822151.

The Walk

1 With your back to the car park entrance, go through the gate in front of you, by the National Trust **Ashridge** sign. There are three grassy paths ahead of you. Take either the left-hand path or the one that goes over the top of grassy knoll – they both come out in the same place. Keep straight ahead, following the black marker post. At the signpost by the gate, on your left, follow the sign straight ahead for the **Ridgeway Bridleway** but taking the right-hand fork of the two grassy trails in front of you. There may be livestock grazing in these fields. Follow this path along the ridge, around the right-hand edge of the hillside. You'll see Chalk Pit water off to your right.

2 At the black marker post with the acorn (where the grassy path bears left) follow the blue arrow straight ahead on the path that goes downhill. Stay on this track around the edge of the escarpment, with **Chalk Pit water** on your right, heading downhill towards some woodland.

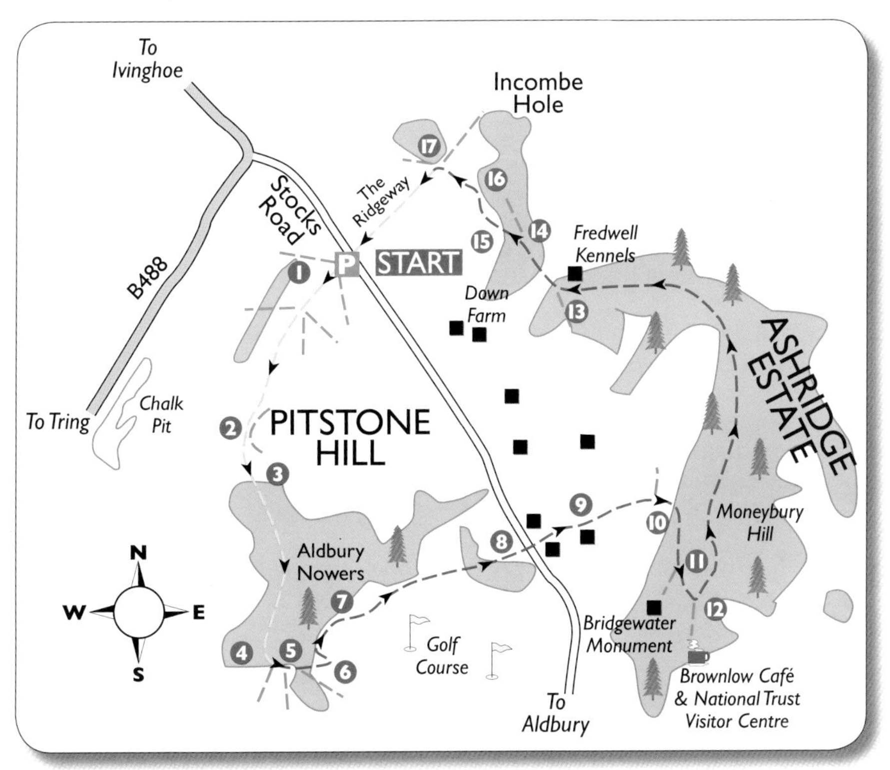

3 At the edge of the wood follow the **Ridgeway** signpost through the gate and into the woods (Aldbury Nowers). Follow this path ahead.

4 After about 750 m the path bears left, down a few rough wooden steps, and then passes through a clearing. It then re-enters the woodland where you'll see a marker post to your left. Follow the main path ahead (bearing slightly to your right) and downhill, and down a series of wooden steps. Ignore the next footpath signpost (indicating right) and keep going to the next signpost, which has several options.

5 Turn left at this signpost (leaving the **Ridgeway**) and follow the footpath sign, along the track heading slightly uphill through the trees. Now keep straight ahead (ignoring the fork to your right after a short distance).

6 Go through the gate and turn left (signposted 6th tee) and follow the track along the trees at the edge of the golf course. After a short distance it bears right and then continues ahead, hugging the tree line.

7 After about 200 m the grassy track departs from the tree-line. Follow it as it bears right (ignoring the track on your left that heads uphill alongside the trees) along the edge of the golf course. Stay on this track as it rejoins the tree-line, keeping straight ahead as it re-enters some woodland, eventually with a fence on your right, until you reach a gate at the road.

8 With your dog on a lead cross the road, following the signpost and go through the gate opposite into the farmyard. Go straight on with the farm buildings on your left and onto a track that leads slightly uphill.

9 At the marker post with the blue arrow, at the corner of the field, keep straight ahead on the bridleway towards the woodland.

10 At the corner of the next field, the main track bears left but keep straight ahead, on the path that leads up through the trees. As it enters the woodland the path bears right and starts a long, fairly steep climb up **Moneybury Hill**.

11 About half-way up the hill, the path forks near a house. The bridleway continues to the right but you'll take the footpath to the left, marked "No Horses".

12 As you near the top of the hill, the path bears left and meets a wide track at a marker post. To visit the **Bridgewater Monument** and **Brownlow Café**, turn right for about 350 m. But to continue on the walk, turn left and

follow the wide track straight ahead through the woodland for the best part of 1.25 miles / 2 km.

13 The path eventually bears left and emerges from the woods to a gate by **Fredwell Kennels**. Keep straight ahead here, then bearing right and downhill.

14 At the bottom of the hill, at the marker post, leave the main track and take the left fork (**Ashridge Estate Boundary Trail**). Follow this path downhill to a gate.

15 Go through the gate (sheep may be grazing after this point) and stay on the path heading downhill, which soon emerges from the woods.

16 At the bottom of the hill, by the corner of the field, bear left, following the fence on your left-hand side.

17 After 200 m, by the black signpost at the next corner of the field, turn left to follow the **Ridgeway** trail (with the fence still on your left) back to the road and car park.

Ivinghoe Beacon

This stunning walk takes in the chalk grasslands of the Ivinghoe Hills Nature Reserve and Ashridge Estate. It incorporates the final leg of the Ridgeway National Trail, which ends at Ivinghoe Beacon, in the north-east tip of the Chiltern Hills. There are far-reaching views over several counties, so this walk is best enjoyed on a calm, sunny day. The area is a

Site of Special Scientific Interest (SSSI) and an Area of Outstanding National Beauty (AONB). The beacon is the site of an Iron Age settlement and the area has been grazed by livestock since prehistoric times. Sheep and cattle are still very much in evidence here (so use a lead in areas where your dog must be under control), though there's still lots of space for running off-lead. During the spring and summer there are many wild flowers, butterflies and birds.

Dog factors

Distance: 2.5 miles / 4.1 km.
Road Walking: None.
Livestock: Yes, cattle and sheep. You will need to put your dog on a lead for parts of the walk but the views and location are second to none.
Stiles: None.
Nearest Vets: Springwell Vets, 98 Western Road, Tring HP23 4BJ ☎ 01442 822151.

Terrain

Open grassland, arable fields, scrub and woodland are all encountered on this walk. There are a couple of steep hill climbs and some paths through the woodland are fairly muddy in winter.

Where to park

Large car park off the road between Ringshall and Ivinghoe (GR 964159).
OS map: Explorer 181 Chiltern Hills North.

How to get there

From Ivinghoe village take the B489 towards Dunstable. After 0.9 miles / 1.4 km turn right, following the brown sign to Ivinghoe Beacon. After 0.7 miles / 1.2 km you'll find a large car park on your left-hand side. Take care as there may be sheep on the road! Postcode HP4 1NF.

Nearest refreshments

Ivinghoe Beacon is the perfect place for a picnic but the Rose & Crown (☎ 01296 668472) in Vicarage Lane, Ivinghoe is an independent free house serving real ales and, at lunchtime on weekends, light refreshments. It has a sunny courtyard and welcomes children and dogs (on a lead) inside, at the bar, and out. Postcode: LU7 9EQ www.roseandcrownivinghoe.com

The Walk

1. There are a few gates leading off from the car park. Look for the one that is approximately in the middle. There is a small sign on the gate reading "Donated by Dunstable Rotary Club". Go through the gate and take the grassy path immediately ahead of you, heading steeply downhill into the valley. After about 100 m, the path crosses a track. Turn left here, along the track, and follow it ahead. As you approach the bottom of the hill, the path bears left towards a gate (donated by the Dunstable Bogtrotters) in the corner of the field.

2. Go through the gate and follow the track (Ashridge Estate Boundary Trail) along the edge of the field, and then across the middle of the field, roughly heading towards a large phone mast in the distance.

3. At the stand of trees, where several fields meet, turn left up the track towards the brow of the hill. Go through the gate on your way up, keeping straight ahead. There may be cattle grazing in this field.

4. At the brow of the hill (with a gate on your right) turn left to walk along the grassy ridge trail, towards **Ivinghoe Beacon**. Keep straight on, through another gate donated by the Dunstable Bogtrotters. Sheep are likely to be grazing in the following fields.

5. At **Ivinghoe Beacon** there are two small stone monuments. After admiring the view, with your back to the monuments, take the grassy track that leads away from the Beacon (**Ridgeway** trail). It soon descends steeply downhill. Keep straight ahead, ignoring all paths off, passing just to the left of a grassy knoll and down to the road.

6. Cross the road to the track on the other side (signposted Ridgeway footpath and Tring Station) and head uphill. You may still encounter sheep in this section of the walk.

7. After only 40 m, leave the main chalky track and take the right-hand fork to follow the **Ridgeway** trail. Follow this track uphill to a gate.

8. Go through the gate and you'll see a sign telling you that the area was once used for military training. Stay on the path straight ahead.

9. After about 200 m, the path peters out into a small area of grassy tufts surrounded by gorse scrub. Turn left here, taking one of the small paths

20

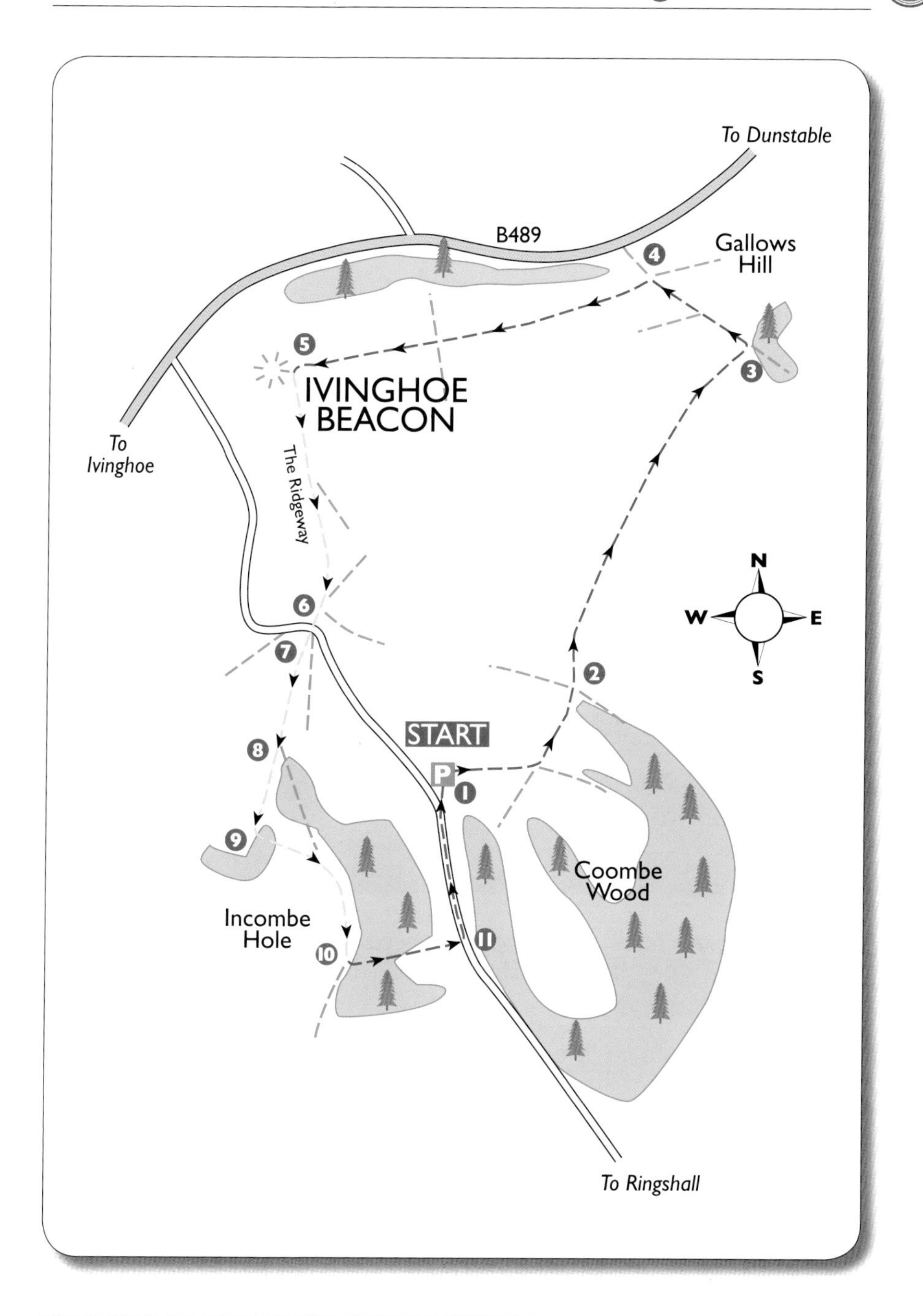
To Dunstable
B489
Gallows Hill
4
3
5
IVINGHOE BEACON
To Ivinghoe
The Ridgeway
N
W
E
S
6
7
2
START
8
P
1
9
Coombe Wood
Incombe Hole
10
11
To Ringshall

through the gorse onto open grassland. Keep straight ahead and you'll soon see the sharp drop of **Incombe Hole** on your right and a gate ahead of you, leading into the woodland.

10 Go through the gate by Incombe Hole (by the stand with the painted rural scene) and take the path directly in front of you through the woodland. It emerges onto an open chalky area of grass with the road in front of you. Turn left and walk back along the road to the main car park.

APPENDIX

The following vets are located close to the walks:

Abivale Veterinary Group
16 Queens Avenue, Wallingford OX10 0ND
www.abivale.com/wallingford ☎ 01491 839043

Abivale Veterinary Group
Belmont Surgery, Belmont, Wantage OX12 9AS www.abivale.com/wantage ☎ 01235 770333

Crossroads Veterinary Centre
36c Couching Street, Watlington OX49 5QQ www.vetswycombe.co.uk ☎ 01491 612799

Drove Veterinary Hospital
Unit 5 Borough Fields, Royal Wootton Bassett SN4 7AX
www.drovevets.co.uk ☎ 01793 852466

Drove Veterinary Hospital
252 Croft Road, Swindon SN1 4RW www.drovevets.co.uk ☎ 01793 522483

Eastcott Veterinary Clinic
6 Clive Parade, Cricklade Road, Swindon SN2 1AJ www.eastcottvets.co.uk ☎ 01793 528341

Goring Veterinary Centre
17C High Street, Goring-On-Thames, RG8 9AR www.fullyvetted.co.uk ☎ 01491 873638

Hall Place Veterinary Centre
1A Dodds Corner, New Road, Stokenchurch HP14 3RZ
www.hallplaceveterinarycentre.co.uk ☎ 01494 485855

Larkmead Veterinary Group
111-113 Park Road, Didcot OX11 8QT www.larkmead.co.uk ☎ 01235 814991

Macqueen Veterinary Centre
1 Waller Road, Devizes SN10 2GH www.macqueenvets.com ☎ 01380 728505

Springwell Vets
98 Western Road, Tring HP23 4BJ www.springwellvets.com ☎ 01442 822151

Sprinz & Nash
Wellington House Veterinary Surgery, Aylesbury Road, Princes Risborough HP27 0JP
www.sprinzandnash.org.uk ☎ 01844 345655

The Veterinary Surgery
21-23 High Street, Stanford-in-the-Vale SN7 8LH
www.vets-surgery.com ☎ 01367 710595

Wendover Heights Veterinary Centre
Tring Road, Halton HP22 5PN
www.whvc.co.uk ☎ 01296 623439